Quarterly Essay 61: Balancing Act

George Megalogenis

16
EasyRead Large

RHYW

Copyright Page from the Original Book

Quarterly Essay is published four times a year by Black Inc., an imprint of Schwartz Publishing Pty Ltd. Publisher: Morry Schwartz.

ISBN 978-1-86395-811-0 ISSN 1832-0953

Subscriptions – 1 year print & digital (4 issues): $79.95 within Australia incl. GST. Outside Australia $119.95. 2 years print & digital (8 issues): $129.95 within Australia incl. GST. 1 year digital only: $39.95.

Payment may be made by Mastercard or Visa, or by cheque made out to Schwartz Publishing. Payment includes postage and handling.

To subscribe, fill out and post the subscription card or form inside this issue, or subscribe online:

www.quarterlyessay.com
subscribe@blackincbooks.com
Phone: 61 3 9486 0288

Correspondence should be addressed to:

The Editor, Quarterly Essay
Level 1, 221 Drummond Street
Carlton VIC 3053 Australia
Phone: 61 3 9486 0288 / Fax: 61 3 9011 6106
Email: quarterlyessay@blackincbooks.com

Editor: Chris Feik. Management: Caitlin Yates. Publicity: Anna Lensky. Design: Guy Mirabella. Assistant Editor: Kirstie Innes-Will. Production Coordinator: Siân Scott-Clash. Typesetting: Tristan Main.

Printed in Australia by McPherson's Printing Group. The paper used to produce this book comes from wood grown in sustainable forests.

BALANCING ACT

Australia Between Recession and Renewal

George Megalogenis

Australia is in transition. Saying it is easy. The panic kicks in when we are compelled to describe what the future might look like. There is no complacent middle to aim at. We will either catch the next wave of prosperity, or finally succumb to the Great Recession.

Each force that is pulling apart our present reads like a turgid unit in a university degree. The technological revolution. Population ageing. The Asian century. Global warming. The mining boom, and bust. The crisis in capitalism. What are the challenges and opportunities? Discuss.

Some of our leaders have revelled in the detail. Kevin Rudd wanted to be across every subject, although he couldn't stick to any one topic long enough for the public to catch up. The annoying imprecision of his method sent his successors to the other extreme of simplicity. It will be impossible for coming generations to separate the banalities of Julia Gillard from those of Tony Abbott. "Moving forward" and "Stop the boats" will be slogans shorn of their contexts, and our children will wonder if our prime ministers were really that shallow. No, they were the most talented politicians of their era, their old supporters will reply. It was just that governing was impossible in the digital age.

Malcolm Turnbull brings us back to where we started with Kevin07 – this is a leader who sounds unafraid of the future. But we are no closer to understanding where the world is heading, or our place in it. We do know we want to remain affluent and egalitarian. Turnbull had that platitude worked out before he took over. He told us on the day he sought the Liberal leadership last September that he wants Australia "to remain a high-wage, generous social-welfare net, first-world society." But in making that pledge, he acknowledged the root of our anxiety: the fear that we will be overrun by globalisation once China no longer has any need for our coal and iron ore.

The national mood has been defensive for so many years now that it is hard to recall the last time we were genuinely free of hang-ups and could look to the future with optimism. We greeted the new millennium as the cheery hosts of the Sydney Olympics, but virtually every message we have sent to the world since then has betrayed our parochialism. The *Tampa* episode of 2001 marked the birth of a long, complex phase of Australian insularity. Its first peak had nothing to do with asylum seekers. It came a few years after the *Tampa,* when the boats had stopped and the mining boom was underway. John Howard gave back every windfall dollar in the budget so that we could treat ourselves. That was the more revealing expression of our self-absorption, unprompted by a global crisis. We simply didn't care enough about the future to reinvest some of that money on behalf of our children. But then Howard double-crossed voters with his WorkChoices program, and the true source of our anger was confirmed – it was globalisation itself. With WorkChoices, Howard reminded Australians that their government no longer felt obliged to defend them against the open economy. Rudd's election win in 2007 briefly broke the spell. We applauded his handling of the global financial crisis, but once the danger had passed he lost his governing nerve, and a new cycle of narcissism commenced. The boats returned in 2009, reviving the old Australian dread of foreign invasion. Abbott ultimately turned the asylum seekers back again with the help of Labor's more punitive policies, but still we were miserable, with him in particular and the world in general.

The supposed strengths of the Australian character – our openness, our love of technology, our pluck – have been notably absent in our attitude to the future. Put bluntly, we don't have a plan. We know we need one, written jointly across government, business, trade unions and civil society. But we keep finding excuses to return to the trenches of our prejudice. Even there, within the sanctuary of the tribe, there is little cohesion. The Liberal Party is split along fault-lines of ideology and personality. Labor still lacks purpose. The trade unions divide between the ineffective and the corrupt. Within my own profession, the media, too many commentators have assigned themselves to covering their rivals. News Corp, for instance, deploys more resources to attacking the ABC than analysing the economy. Only business appears to have unity of purpose in its relentless pursuit of concessions from government.

The most consistent message sent by voters to the main parties over the past decade and a half has been the demand for security. Both sides have taken this to mean border protection and bribes at the ballot box; one fist clenched against the rest of the world, while the other hand offers cash to the most aggrieved. Yet each leader that tried this was bewildered when voters could not be appeased. The truth is that the demand for security is more sophisticated than politics has allowed. We want our leaders to think for the long term; to prepare us for life beyond the mining boom. Both sides have found this in their research since the earliest days of the boom, but both have been unable to see past the next Newspoll. Something deeper is happening here than the predictable incompetence of politics. The system knows what voters are really asking for: a return to some form of government intervention in the economy. Yet this is resisted because of a misguided faith in the open economic model. The only leader who seriously tried to find a way out of the impasse was Rudd, but he lost focus after the global financial crisis. Now a Liberal prime minister is being asked by the public to redraw the line between the market and the state.

The economy was the primary reason Turnbull gave for challenging Abbott. "It is clear enough that the government is not successful in providing the economic leadership that we need," he declared.

> It is not the fault of individual ministers. Ultimately the prime minister has not been capable of providing the economic leadership our nation needs; he has not been capable of providing the economic confidence that business needs ... The big economic changes that we're living through here and around the world offer enormous challenges and enormous opportunities and we need a different style of leadership. We need a style of leadership that ... explains the challenges and how to seize the opportunities. A style of leadership that respects the people's intelligence ... We need advocacy, not slogans.

He wasn't pitching to undecided colleagues, because the numbers to topple Abbott were already locked in. This assessment was delivered for the benefit of the public, and six months after the coup it remains the most remarkable admission that a Coalition government has made while in office.

No previous regime removed its leader on grounds of economic incompetence, although others probably should have. Before Abbott, the conservatives had replaced three sitting prime ministers – Billy Hughes in 1923, Robert Menzies in 1941 and John Gorton in 1971. In each case, the basic complaint was leadership style: arrogance, in short.

With Abbott, the personal and the polling were secondary to economic management. His erratic, uninspiring leadership demoralised business and consumers to an extent that no prime minister had since Gough Whitlam. Confidence in the future is the essential ingredient of economic growth. For a nation in transition, a loss of confidence can create a self-fulfilling prophecy of missed opportunities. Businesses become risk-averse. Consumers close their wallets. Employers respond to that weaker demand by cutting costs. Workers react to the squeeze on their wages by reducing spending. And so on, until growth stalls.

It was on Abbott's watch that we finally lost our global economic bragging right. The verdict was confirmed on the very day he was ousted, 14 September 2015, when the International Monetary Fund released its annual review of the Australian economy. "Australia has enjoyed exceptionally strong income growth for the past two decades," the IMF concluded. "But the waning resource investment boom and sharp fall in the terms of trade have brought this to a halt. A cyclical recovery is likely in the near term, but over the medium term, income growth is likely to slow to a rate in line with other advanced economies."

Identifying when Australia's long run of economic over-achievement ended is relatively easy. It was June 2014, when our unemployment rate crossed 6 per cent for the first time in eleven years. Timing matters here. This was just one month after the release of the Abbott government's pugnacious first budget. Unemployment had been creeping up in the final year of the Rudd – Gillard government. The economy needed support. But the new regime was screaming "budget emergency" and even though the Senate blocked the most contentious cuts, the announcement alone was sufficient to push unemployment over the 6 per cent threshold. The unusual part of this story is that unemployment rose despite the recovery in the United States. This had never happened before. The Australian and American unemployment rates had moved in the same direction, up or down, since at least the 1940s, reflecting the gravitational pull of the world's largest economy. That connection held throughout the mining boom, and even in the Great Recession itself. A revival in the United States should have lifted activity in Australia, but this time it didn't.

The media post-mortems did consider the role that the 2014 budget played in Abbott's removal, but very little attention was given to the damage it did to the economy. "The defining economic event of the government's life was its first budget," Peter Hartcher wrote in a five-part series of articles for the Fairfax newspapers. "[It] 'brought the government to the brink of destruction' as Abbott later conceded privately."

> From the time that budget was delivered, the Abbott government was fated to never again lead in the polls. It was overreach on a monumental scale and broke all the rules of political management – the government broke promises, had no mandate, failed to prepare public opinion, and misjudged the Senate and public opinion so profoundly that most of its hallmark measures became moribund, at a dead end in the Senate.

This is where the analysis stopped: at the marketing. The article was not designed to assess the individual measures; it was a news feature, not an economic think-piece. But it was typical of the weight the media placed on the personal and political when cataloging the many disappointments of the Abbott government. (To be fair, journalists had an embarrassment of anecdotes to distract them.)

This focus on the personal and political meant that a discredited government had the final word on the question of economic competence. Abbott and his supporters were free to maintain the illusion that the policies blocked by the Senate were in the national interest. They would only plead guilty to the lesser crime of poor salesmanship. Joe Hockey, the treasurer who failed to pass that first budget, used his farewell speech to parliament to chide everyone but himself.

"Mr Speaker, the Abbott government was good at policy but struggled with politics ... I admit that we could have done more to win over third-party endorsements and to win over the Senate; and we could have done more to win over the Australian people." It was a Clayton's contrition. He concluded this section of his valedictory by asserting that "the government had more courage than the parliament."

Hockey had the humility to depart politics. Abbott remained, extending his festival of self-pity into an election year. In defending his record, Abbott claimed to be supporting Turnbull's government. Not even Rudd was this crass. And so the question of competence which Turnbull raised is yet to be addressed. It is resisted outright by the minority of commentators who cling to Abbott, and it is overlooked by the rest of the media, who, like the public at large, are relieved to see the back of another divisive prime minister. Whether consciously or otherwise, many journalists, indeed many public servants, business chiefs and probably the majority of the electorate, view Turnbull as the solution to the crisis he identified. He is the grown-up who will terminate the Rudd – Gillard – Abbott era. This is flattering, perhaps, for a politician with a high opinion of himself, but unhelpful for a prime minister who wants to restore faith in government and reinvigorate Australian capitalism. Voters don't just want a return to adult government; they crave new ideas, so that the future does not seem so intimidating.

Our political history offers little comfort to Turnbull, because the governments which transformed the economy in the past were Labor, not conservative. The first was led by John Curtin, the second by Bob Hawke. Both had treasurers who were their equal, and who succeeded them as prime minister. In each case, Labor had consciously changed its governing culture in response to a global catastrophe. The key members of the Curtin – Chifley government lived through the collapse of Jim Scullin's Labor government during the darkest years of the Great Depression. The Hawke – Keating ministry witnessed the implosion of Gough Whitlam's government. On both occasions, Labor remade itself in Opposition before it returned to power.

To inspire a similar transformation in a Coalition government, Turnbull has to convince his colleagues they have already failed in office. They can't pretend that their former leader was an anomaly – a poor communicator with a brilliant program – because it was the conservative agenda for small government which undermined confidence.

Labor and now Liberal have made the same inexcusable blunder. They took the shortcut to power without the necessary policy renewal in Opposition. When they found governing much harder than expected, they turned to what they knew best – politics – and removed a first-term prime minister. Policy renewal could wait until after they had secured re-election with a new leader. The question for

Turnbull is whether he can buy enough time to reset the system. One three-year term surely won't be enough. He has to correct for policy errors on the conservative side running across two decades – the six most wasteful years of the Howard government from 2001 to 2007, and the six combative years when Abbott led the Liberal Party from 2009 to 2015. The way government is run has to change along with the substance of policy. Turnbull conceded this point on the day of the challenge. "We need to restore traditional cabinet government," he said. "There must be an end to policy on the run and captain's calls. We need to be truly consultative with colleagues, members of parliament, senators and the wider public. We need an open government." For that to happen, Turnbull has to give up some of the self-defeating powers that his predecessors accumulated in the prime minister's office.

The tabloid critique of Abbott, and indeed Rudd, is that they were bonkers. It is made by MPs who claimed to be aware of their idiosyncrasies before casting a leadership ballot for them. Conveniently, they assumed these men would modify their behaviour after they won an election. The fulfilment of ambition, and the responsibility of government, was supposed to turn Abbott and Rudd into statesmen. Instead, success made them unaccountable. Both men challenged the very system they served by elevating their personal offices above the ministry and caucus. They behaved like presidents. It is uncanny how

Turnbull's eloquent call to restore cabinet government echoed Gillard's plodding justification for taking Rudd's job five years earlier: a good government had lost its way.

Abbott and Rudd were not bad at politics. On the contrary, they were masters of campaigning, so skilled that they rewrote the rules. Abbott was elected prime minister despite his unpopularity. Rudd was the first Labor leader to win office when the economy was strong. Both men made perfect sense in Opposition, yet repeated their predecessor's mistakes. Rudd nailed Howard for wasting the proceeds of the mining boom, and then lost control of the budget after the global financial crisis. Abbott mocked the Rudd and Gillard soap opera, and then governed by yelling. Was either side actually paying attention in Opposition?

What these driven individuals could not grasp, refused even to countenance, was that an Australian prime minister does not have the formal power of a president. A president is directly elected by the people. This provides security of tenure. A president can only be removed by Congress in the most extraordinary circumstances. The US House of Representatives has impeached just two, at the rate of one per century: Andrew Johnson in 1868 and Bill Clinton in 1998. Both were acquitted by the Senate. Australian prime ministers are elected by the party room, and although they have more effective power than a president because they usually control the House of Representatives, they can be dismissed without warning when their colleagues fear losing office. A rapid turnover of leaders is not a recent affliction of our system. From the moment the Australian colonies were granted self-government in the 1850s, the most precarious position in the parliament was that of premier. In the first decade of federation, Australia swapped prime ministers seven times – from Barton to Deakin, then Watson, Reid, Deakin, Fisher, Deakin and Fisher. Only the first departure was voluntary. The next five changes occurred on the floor of the House of Representatives.

On a superficial level, the Rudd – Gillard – Abbott era matched the chaos. There were five prime ministers between 2010 and 2015, with only one change occurring at the ballot box, in 2013. But there was a crucial difference. In the federation's formative years, there was continuity in policy, from leader to leader, and from party to party. Deakin and Fisher were aligned on the biggest questions of the day: industry protection and the settling of wages through arbitration. (The sole exception was George Reid's Free Trade Party, which ruled for ten months between 1904 and 1905.)

With Rudd, Gillard and Abbott, entire programs were thrown out with the leader. And on the most vexing issue of all, climate change, each leader took several different positions. John Howard was no better. In government, he was an advocate for the original Kyoto protocol on climate change before he became an opponent, and was against emissions trading before he was for it.

I have no doubt that Rudd and Abbott sincerely believed their centralised approach was necessary, because their parties stood for little more than acquiring power. Ideas had to come from somewhere, and so it made sense to generate the big ones out of the prime minister's office. Rudd immersed himself in the paperwork. Abbott relied on his gut. But their decision-making was compromised by a shared insecurity. They wanted to be the smartest guy in the room, and so they cleared it of contrary viewpoints. Inevitably, policies became associated with the leader, not the party.

The danger of throwing out policies along with the leader can be seen in how Gillard dealt with the mining tax. To prove that she was not Rudd, and that she could cut a deal with the mining companies, Gillard allowed them to design their own tax.

To date, Turnbull has limited the policy repudiation to the soft targets of his predecessor's obsessions. He terminated Abbott's imperial honours system, lifted the veto on wind farms, and declared the federal government once more willing to fund public transport infrastructure, science and innovation. No doubt he wants to do more, but is wary of giving Abbott a right of reply this side of an election.

The difficulty for Turnbull, indeed for the entire system, is that too much is expected of the prime minister. The rhythm of politics today is the permanent volatility of the financial market. Messiah bubbles form around individuals, then burst. Then the speculators move on to the next saviour. Labor's Kevin07 campaign was the prototype for the leader as superhero. Rudd was the policy nerd who would restore serious government after the cynicism of Howard, and the Mandarin speaker who would keep the Chinese onside. A similar set of qualities has been projected onto Turnbull. He is the suave intellect who will counter the small-mindedness of Abbott, and the merchant banker who will tame globalisation on our behalf. If the Rudd experience is any guide, Turnbull may remain popular for quite some time, because the public is willing him to succeed. But this type of political celebrity can be a trap. The Rudd bubble ultimately burst because he would not lead. One non-decision was enough for people to write him off. When Rudd dumped his emissions trading scheme, voters concluded that he was just another politician.

On the previous two occasions when Australia reinvented itself, in the 1940s and 1980s, it was taken for granted that the project would be collaborative. Strong bonds of trust existed between politics, bureaucracy and the press, and between the representatives of labour, capital and welfare. Those connections have been broken by a culture that favours the attention-seeker over the expert, and the bully over the consensus-builder.

The debate we have to have is on the role of government in the economy. It is being forced on us by the market failures of the twenty-first century. Both sides cling defensively to the open model because it tells them a reassuring story of Australian success. But that open model has been exhausted by capitalism's extended crisis and the end of the mining boom. It cannot guarantee prosperity in the future without an active state. Once politicians understand this, they can release themselves from the spell cast by the leader they wish to be, Paul Keating.

The open model excels when the economy is strong, and in response to a global shock. But it struggles when the economy is in transition, because the market forces it is responding to are compromised. The four components of the model are a floating currency, low tariffs, interest rates set independently of the government, and wages determined directly by employer and workers above a minimum standard. Each is now delivering perverse results that are actually increasing the risk of recession.

For an uncomfortable period in 2012, and again in 2014, it seemed that the Australian dollar would not follow commodity prices down, leaving non-mining businesses gasping for air. The American car-makers used our overvalued currency as their excuse to quit the Australian market altogether.

The goals of low tariffs were to flush out uncompetitive firms and release investment for globally minded businesses. It worked in the 1990s, but then mining crowded out all other activity. The boom ran from late 2003 to late 2011, with a brief pause during the global financial crisis. Now, on the other side of the mining cycle, investment is moving to the least productive part of the economy: housing. In normal times, the open model would respond with one, maybe two small rises in interest rates and a stern lecture from the governor of the Reserve Bank to prevent the market from overheating. But our central bank is hostage to a global experiment in very low interest rates designed to prop up the US and European economies. Those very low interest rates have seen property prices surge in Sydney. Any Australian politician who grasps the basics of our economic history should appreciate the danger of a housing bubble. Yet there has been a curious lack of engagement with this threat.

The final flaw in the open model is the enterprise bargaining system. It is excessively stingy at the moment because the balance of power has shifted too far towards the employer. In 2015 workers in the private sector received their smallest pay rise since the wages system was deregulated by Paul Keating. Surging house prices coupled with a squeeze on disposable incomes are the preconditions for a bust, but the open model can't resolve the conundrum.

A lever is missing, and it is one that governments forgot they still have control of: fiscal policy – the taxes they raise or lower, and the money they spend or invest. Fiscal policy briefly came back into fashion during the global financial crisis – in the form of the cash payments to consumers and the schools building program – only to fall out of favour again when Labor and the Coalition had a bipartisan panic attack over the budget deficit. Each side then pretended the crisis was over. Aggressive, then passive; these bewildering shifts in rhetoric from the treasurers became as unsettling as the sloganeering of the prime ministers.

All the elements of the open model operated with textbook efficiency in the global financial crisis. The currency tumbled, interest rates were slashed and employers spared their workers from mass retrenchment by reducing the hours they worked. The Rudd government's cash handouts were effective because they complemented these measures. The need for fiscal policy now is to relieve the open model from a burden it was never designed for – managing an economy in transition. I am not arguing for stimulus to tide us over until capitalism resolves its crisis, but for a permanent change in the relationship between the state and the market. Government must reclaim responsibility for the areas of public policy that will prepare us for the future – most notably, education and infrastructure.

As a journalist I am wary of giving advice, especially when it involves a greater role for government in the economy. I can think of no generation of politicians I would trust less with the responsibility of redrawing the line between the market and the state than the current crop. But the choice is being forced on Australia anyway. The political system cannot restore public confidence without a more responsive government. And the economy won't stabilise without a more active government. The default setting of politics in the twenty-first century – to trust in the market – has proven to be bad economics, even for Australia, the only high-income nation to avoid the Great Recession. It has left us with gridlocked cities, growing inequality and a corporate sector that feels no obligation to pay tax. If politics waits any longer to address these issues, we will muddle into a recession and government will have to prop up the economy, but from a position of weakness, with the budget in deficit and interest rates too low to cut in a meaningful way.

This essay will explore how to augment the open model, based on the experience of the past fifteen years. The first step is to identify what is driving the big economic and cultural shifts of the era, both local and global. The changes are best understood by dividing the economy into its male and female sides.

NATION-BUILDING

The Australian male has had a prosperous twenty-first century so far. Ignore the white-guy whinge about how women, and the Chinese, and the Indians, are pushing him to the sidelines of the culture. The unexpected story of the past decade and a half is the return of the full-time male worker. More than 1.6 million full-time jobs were created between 2000 and 2015, and for the first time since the 1960s the majority of those positions (more than 900,000) went to men.

The turnaround is not directly explained by the resources boom. The main engine of growth was construction, which was responsible for 300,000 of the 900,000 new full-time male jobs. Mining can claim an indirect stake in this activity through the many projects it generated, from the quarry to the port. But the greater influence was the residential property boom, which commenced in 1999, around four years before the rise of China. This should not come as a surprise.

It is the identity of the next largest employer which challenges the old assumption that the male side of the economy relies on brawn. More than 200,000 full-time male jobs were created in professional, scientific and technical services. These winners of the open economy include accountants, architects, computer programmers, lawyers, managers and scientific researchers. The number would have been even larger had the Australian Bureau of Statistics counted doctors and other medical specialists in this category, instead of in health care and social assistance.

Politics has no language to tell this story. It cuts against the foundation myth of Australia as the worker's paradise, where only men with blue collars need apply to define the nation's centre. White-collar workers comprised less than 4 per cent of male employees when the Hawke – Keating government first opened up the economy in the 1980s. Almost five times as many men worked in manufacturing back then. Manufacturing remained the dominant employer through the tectonic shifts of the 1980s and '90s, but it was losing ground to construction. It finally ceded top spot in 2006, and on present trends will drop to third, behind professional, scientific and technical services, either later this year or in 2017. Ironically, the electoral implications are not appreciated by the professionals of the political class. The main parties still have their eyes fixed on the rearview mirror of Howard's battlers, the term strategists used to describe the blue-collar males who switched from Labor to Liberal or Pauline Hanson in the 1990s. The Abbott government tried to revive them in the form of Tony's tradies, but this narrow macho pitch merely reminded the rest of the population that their prime minister did not relate to them.

The tertiary-educated men and women of Australia – let's call them Malcolm's graduates – are the underestimated voter of the twenty-first century. The main parties have tended to ignore them, despite their growing numbers, because they are assumed to be an alien species with no connection to ordinary Australians. In circular logic that only the political class could come up with, leaders have tried to play the elites off against the majority by talking down to the electorate. All this does is increase cynicism with politics, perpetuating the very problem the main parties were trying to fix – their declining primary vote. The poll numbers only improve when a party courts the blue-collar worker and the professional together, with an optimistic leader like Kevin Rudd or Malcolm Turnbull.

MALE SIDE OF THE ECONOMY

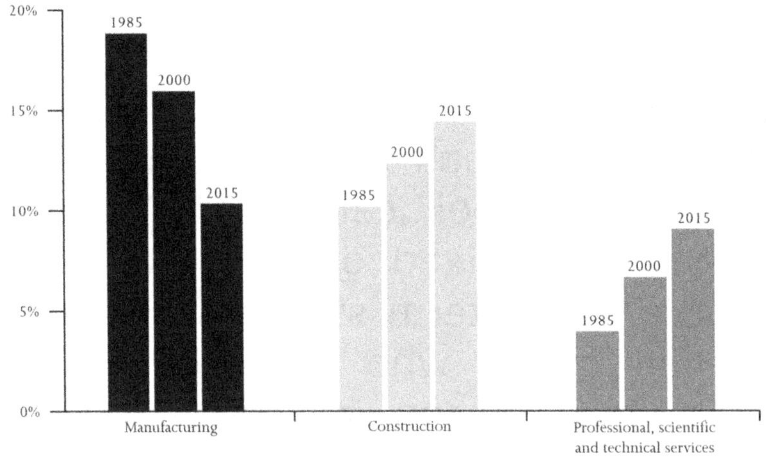

The economics of our fractured modern workforce are even more challenging for the main parties. Although male jobs are diversifying, the concentration of blue-collar workers in construction creates a new set of risks that did not apply behind the tariff wall. Men who lost work in the protection era could expect to be rehired by the same employer, or at least in the same industry, in a recovery. That began to change in the recessions of the mid-1970s and early 1980s. By the early 1990s, the majority of the men who were laid off in that recession either left the workforce for good or became self-employed. The political system could barely contain their rage back then. How will it cope if their sons are laid off, when the main parties already face an existential threat from the Greens, independents and populists?

Construction is usually the first industry to shed staff in a downturn, and if the next recession is triggered by a housing bust, unemployment may climb too quickly for authorities to prevent a hard landing. Lay-offs in construction would set off a chain reaction of job losses in retail, which is already facing a severe challenge from online shopping. No one under the age of forty has any direct experience of the last crash in Australia, and we simply don't know how this generation would respond to a soft or hard landing, given the debts it is carrying. Household debt was 70 per cent of household income in 1990. Today it is more than double that – 185 per cent.

The danger to social cohesion multiplies because the resources boom has already hollowed out other industries. The 140,000 new jobs created in mining since 2000 matched an almost identical loss of jobs in manufacturing. As mining inevitably contracts, where will these men go next? They cannot simply return to their old workplace, because many of those businesses have closed down.

The manufacturing job losses of the past five years are comparable to those caused by the early 1990s recession. Another round of mass retrenchments is likely as Holden and Toyota wind up their Australian operations in 2017. The question the Turnbull government should be asking itself before the property market cools, before Clive Palmer shuts down another venture, and before the car industry disappears, is whether the public sector can find work for tens of thousands of blue-collar men before they become a political wrecking ball.

The answer is to put them to work on major infrastructure projects, restoring government to the part of the economy it should never have abandoned in the name of deregulation. This is one of the magic keys of policy that can unlock Australian potential: public investment in areas such as transport, communications and water security. It might even release politics from its obsessions with media management and factional intrigue. Once the state resumes responsibility for the things the market either can't deliver, or delivers at unreasonable cost to taxpayers, the focus of politics nation-building. Inevitably, some bad decisions will be made with public funds, but the time has long past when that was a plausible reason not to act.

The running down of infrastructure has been a sore point with voters for at least a decade. They understood the economics better than the politicians. As their lives sped up, their communities succumbed to gridlock, slowing the trip from home to work, to school and to the child-care centre. But the system has struggled to correct itself because the capacity of government to invest in the economy has been diminished by years of neglect.

Another monster was created during the government's absence from the real economy. When the main parties embraced the market in the 1980s and '90s by selling public assets and winding back investment in infrastructure, they left an opening where the state once was. The theory was that funds would be freed for more productive investments in the private sector. It was only half-right. Public investment fell from around 8 per cent of gross domestic product in the mid-1980s to around 4 per cent from the late '90s on. Half that opening was filled by business investment, but the other half went to bricks and mortar. This transaction came to define the Howard era, and by the middle of 2000 the property sector was substantially larger than the public sector, contributing a record 6.7 per cent of GDP compared to 4.6 per cent for public investment. In effect, we were building new housing estates and apartment blocks without train lines or schools to service them.

That particular spike in activity was unsustainable, because the industry was trying to beat the introduction of the GST on 1 July 2000. Construction froze in the second half of 2000, and the economy almost went into recession because of it. The message an economist would have drawn from this episode was beware the property cycle. Not John Howard. He doubled the first home owner's grant, and the patient had their fever restored. By 2003, property investment was worth 6.2 per cent of GDP compared to 4.1 per cent for public investment. Housing maintained its lead through the first phase of the mining boom, a distortion Howard further encouraged by returning revenue windfalls to taxpayers, instead of using some of that money for infrastructure.

The global financial crisis was supposed to provide the reset that would bring government back into the field. In the earliest days of the crisis, the Rudd government made an offer to the states it thought would be too good to refuse. Give us your pending list of infrastructure projects and the federal government will help fund them. An embarrassed silence followed. Treasury secretary Ken Henry explains: "Not one government in Australia had even one infrastructure project sitting in its top drawer, ready for investment – not even one." Staggering, because the common complaint of every Labor state regime against the former Howard government was that infrastructure had been short-changed.

Rudd would not be deterred. His second stimulus package, announced in February 2009, contained more cash payments and the most ambitious government infrastructure program since the Snowy Mountains Scheme: the schools building program. It was designed to support construction employment until the crisis had passed, and proved to be quite successful. But at the time it suffered from guilt by association with the pink batts insulation scheme.

I still marvel at Tony Abbott's oppositionist brilliance in 2010. He shifted the blame for a global recession onto the government that had managed to avoid it. All it required was a simple reframing of the argument from jobs saved to money wasted, and for Labor to lose itself in the personality clash between Kevin Rudd and Julia Gillard.

What the schools building program actually achieved, and where it fell short of its promise, should be of interest to policy-makers around the world. It is a perfect case study of government intervention through infrastructure, because the money flowed relatively quickly.

Construction jobs fell by 18,000 in the year after the global financial crisis. Although a relatively small decline by the standards of past recessions, it was nonetheless the first such fall in eight years.

The schools building program could do nothing about those lay-offs. The test is what happened to employment in the following year, and the news was very good. More than 50,000 people were hired. The contribution of the schools building program could also be seen in the national accounts. Public investment had been 5.2 per cent of GDP when the scheme was announced. It increased in each of the next four quarters and peaked at 6.7 per cent in the March quarter of 2010. Private investment collapsed over the same period, from 16.1 per cent of GDP to 14.3 per cent, while housing investment remained more or less steady.

Case closed. Except that Labor could not make that case to the electorate. This meant the Coalition could continue to proclaim the opposite: that Labor had been reckless with public funds. Unfortunately, the Coalition believed its own spin and did not see the need to increase spending.

Tony Abbott took office with private investment at 16.9 per cent of GDP, and public and housing investment each at 4.7 per cent. If he had understood the risk, he would have fast-tracked some infrastructure projects. Instead, he did nothing. Two years later, as Abbott joined Gillard and Rudd in the political past tense, private investment had dropped to 14.1 per cent of GDP and public investment to 4.1 per cent. All that was holding up the investment side of the economy was bricks and mortar, which was being supported by low interest rates. Housing investment reached 5.6 per cent of GDP – its highest level since before the global financial crisis. No matter how many times politicians say they want to invest in the future, they lack the discipline to follow through. Abbott wanted to be known as Australia's infrastructure prime minister, but evinced little interest in the topic while in office.

The tragedy here is that our leaders refuse to learn from experience. The schools building program was policy on the run. It helped the economy in the short term, but was it the most productive investment the government could have made at the time? We don't know because, as Ken Henry says, there wasn't a decent list of projects to choose from.

The IMF chided the Abbott government in 2015 for tightening public spending when the economy needed support. In response to this criticism, according to the IMF, "[the government] concurred that addressing infrastructure bottlenecks was a key priority and funding of high quality infrastructure projects was a key focus. They also pointed to substantial existing planned investments, including the national broadband network, with total general government investment over coming years expected to remain above levels of the 1990s and early 2000s." Kevin Rudd might have afforded himself a chuckle that the NBN was put forward as an example of Coalition intervention.

The scale of the problem is only partly acknowledged in the government's response. Maintaining public investment "above the levels of the 1990s and early 2000s" will not give the nation the infrastructure it needs. If Australia is to catch up, spending should probably return to the levels of the 1960s, when it was closer to 10 per cent of GDP. It is no use pretending that the private sector can deliver physical infrastructure such as rail lines or roads better than the government. The market has had two decades to prove otherwise, and its legacy is congestion. This is not to suggest there is no role for the private sector, or that in areas such as technology or energy the government should revive the old, discredited policy of picking winners. The lines do not need to be redrawn. The existing model – where government provides support for innovation through subsidies, but leaves it to the scientists and other experts to come up with the ideas, and the private sector to bring them to consumers – works well. But government must take the lead on physical infrastructure. Only it has an economy-wide perspective. The market, left to its own devices, will only build houses.

John Howard was fond of asserting that there was no infrastructure crisis in Australia, and even if there was, it was the fault of the Labor states. There was a good deal of truth to the second part of this observation. Responsibility for infrastructure is shared among federal, state and even local governments. The federal government has sole jurisdiction over telecommunications, while electricity, dams, water supply, sewerage, ports and public transport are in the hands of the states. Road and rail are the key areas of overlap, and it is here that the trivial rivalries of federation have caused the greatest economic damage.

The state that claims to have the most innovative policy record in the new millennium also provides the best illustration of what went wrong on infrastructure. Victorians can't say they didn't see the issue coming. The Coalition government of Jeff Kennett and the Labor government of Steve Bracks were a decade ahead of the nation in promoting a high-migration future for their state when every other mainland government was dabbling in Hansonism. Even Bob Carr, the unashamedly cosmopolitan New South Wales premier, played the low-migration card, declaring Sydney full at the turn of the twenty-first century.

Victoria wanted people, yet when they came the Bracks government didn't build fast enough to cater for them. Labor couldn't connect the dots between the realisation of its dream for a big Victoria and the public transport network that would be needed to service it. Money and time were wasted on an infuriating electronic ticketing system, when what the state really needed was to expand Melbourne's train network.

Joel Deane chronicled the mistakes in his book on the Victorian Labor government, *Catch and Kill.* He quotes transport minister Peter Batchelor, who suggests the government had trouble focusing on the biggest issue before it:

> Each year there tended to be an area of government that would do exceptionally well out of the budget. It would be schools one year, or

> hospitals the next, and the metropolitan public transport was left too late and the difficulty with public metropolitan train services [is] they take so long to bring to fruition. So, if you don't start early you never get anywhere near it to compete [with the increased patronage].

Steve Bracks told Deane that the problem began with the state's treasury department consistently underestimating both population growth and the effect this growth would have on passenger numbers.

> Our policy was to lift the use of public transport from 30, 40 per cent, whatever it was, to 80 per cent ... Those targets became totally irrelevant as our population continued to boom and our employment levels continued to grow, which meant people were commuting to jobs in the city.

It was only late in the life of the government that public transport received attention in the budget. But John Brumby, treasurer under Bracks and by now premier, still did not see it as an election-decider. That misreading of community sentiment ensured Labor would lose every seat along the Frankston train line in the 2010 campaign, and with them, office. The new Coalition government did not believe public transport mattered all that much either. Its priority was roads, and in the 2014 election, voters dispatched a second government in a row, returning Labor to power after a single term in Opposition.

By now, the political argument for public investment should roll off the tongue. Infrastructure promotes growth, and maintains social cohesion by keeping people connected. When the economy is weak, it has the bonus of saving jobs.

With experience, governments can use their projects to augment the open model. Spending could be boosted when the private sector is weak. The NBN would be an ideal vehicle for a flexible fiscal policy. However, the Coalition has been slow to take up this opportunity because its tribal instinct is to squeeze the programs of its Labor predecessor in order to free up funds for its own agenda. To date, no level of government has cleared the practical obstacles of project selection and implementation. The electoral cycle runs too quickly for the investment cycle, and until the parties adopt a more mature approach, each new government will be condemned to repeat the errors of its predecessor as it tries to rewrite the nation's infrastructure policy from scratch.

***

The volatility on the male side of the economy can be moderated once government rediscovers the lost art of planning. The policy challenges on the female side are more complex. Job security is not the issue, because as the population ages there will be more work in health care and social assistance. This sector was responsible for one in three of the 1.5 million jobs created for women over the past fifteen years, and is now the single largest employer in the nation.

Note how the economy is distributing labour in every direction. Behind the tariff wall of old Australia, three of the top five employers were working-class and predominantly male – manufacturing, construction and agriculture. Now three of the top five are pink-collar, including the two largest employers. Women hold the majority of jobs in health care and social assistance (80 per cent), retail (55 per cent) and education (70 per cent). Only one of the top five is blue-collar – construction, which is 90 per cent male.

The relative improvement in male full-time work over the past fifteen years has not slowed the feminisation of the workforce. The biggest shift has been from full-time male work to part-time female work. More than 80 per cent of all jobs were full-time when the dollar was floated in December 1983. In the intervening thirty-two years, that proportion has shrunk from 82.6 per cent to 69.1 per cent. Although men still hold the majority of those full-time jobs, they are now outnumbered by all women in work, either full-time or part-time.

What is wrong with this picture is that deregulation has yet to unleash the full potential of the better-educated half of Australian society. Women are marginalised in work, even as they become numerically dominant. Across all sectors, they are still paid less for doing the same work as men, and the jobs the economy is generating for them tend to be at the lower end of the income scale.

There is another aspect to consider. We are one of just three developed nations where part-time work accounts for more than 30 per cent of all jobs. Only the Netherlands and Switzerland have higher rates of casualisation than Australia. In Canada, the economy most like ours, part-time work is just under 20 per cent; in New Zealand it is below 25 per cent. Our settler cousins also boast notably higher rates of female employment than ours.

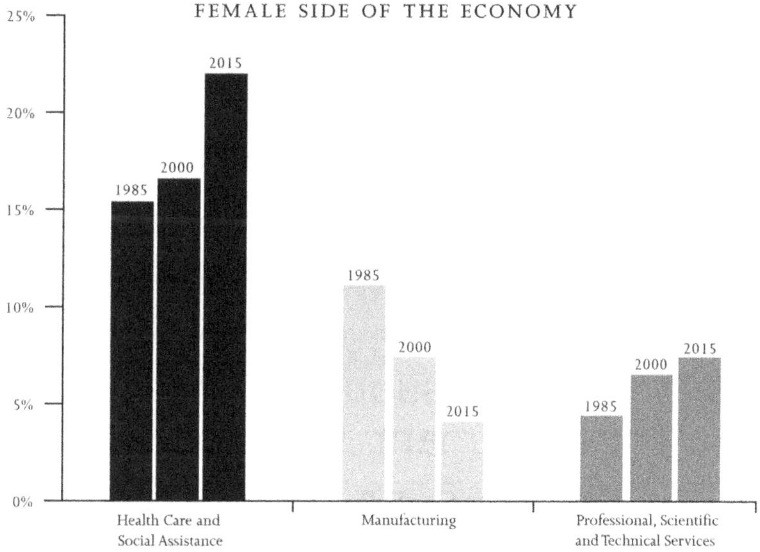

An optimist would read these differences as an opportunity. If Australia could move its female employment rate up to match Canada's, and reduce its casualisation rate towards New Zealand's, the boost to the economy would be substantial. But what if these differences reflect a national hang-up about gender? Australia's political culture remains doggedly macho. Tony Abbott could only find room for one woman in his first nineteen-member cabinet, Canada's conservative leader Stephen Harper had six out of twenty-six when he took office in 2006. Malcolm Turnbull's first cabinet had five women out of twenty-one, again well short of the new Canadian standard of fifteen out of thirty-one under Prime Minister Justin Trudeau. Asked why he wanted gender equality, Trudeau replied: "Because it is 2015." By their own example, the governments of Abbott and Turnbull devalue female participation in work. To close the gap with our peers, politics may first need to undergo its own feminisation, so the ministry and the wider parliament more closely resemble the society they serve.

Australia's high rates of part-time work reveal a further uncomfortable truth about the open economy: the pendulum swing of power from labour to capital. Employer associations have been beating their chests for decades about the supposed high cost of labour in Australia. The argument was valid in the Whitlam – Fraser era, when wages surged to historic highs and profits were reduced to their lowest level as a proportion of national income on record. Wages accounted for more than 60 per cent of national income between 1974 and 1978 and again in 1982–83. Both episodes were associated with industrial mayhem and deep recessions, and they have distorted the conservative view of the world ever since. I lost count of the number of stories my old newspaper, the

Australian, and its rival the *Australian Financial Review* ran under the headline "Wages breakout." There was never any data to support the scare.

The open model was designed to restore the profits of employers, and on any impartial reading of the evidence it has overshot. In the full employment 1960s, business profits averaged 20 per cent of national income. In each decade of deregulation, the profit share has been above that, averaging 24 per cent at the end of the 1980s, 25 per cent in the 1990s, 26 per cent on the eve of the global financial crisis and spiking to 28 per cent with the second mining boom. Each percentage point gain for capital has been at the expense of labour.

Yet the urge to blame the worker has not passed. Weekend penalty rates are a favourite target. Hotels and restaurants claim more of them would open for business on Sundays if they could pay their staff the weekday rate. Perhaps, but it does not follow that the economy would be better off, let alone the young waiter whose take-home pay is likely to be cut. Household consumption is the beating heart of any economy. It accounts for more than half of Australia's GDP, and should not be restricted without good reason. Accommodation and food services employ more than 800,000 workers. Many would be worse off without penalty rates. Their loss of spending power would need to be at least matched by greater consumption by the rest of the population to leave the economy no worse off. I can't see it happening in the present environment. What has been holding back households since the global financial crisis is not the lack of opportunities to spend, but the debts they are carrying. A seventh day of consumption might help cafés, but the money that flows there will be offset by cutbacks on other discretionary items.

This is a small example of a one-sided conversation between the business lobby and the public. There is virtually no support in the community for the abolition of weekend penalty rates. Not even Tony Abbott would fly this flag for business. But the open model has indulged capital to the point where it confuses its own pecuniary interest with the national good.

One of the most glaring manifestations of this is the salaries that company executives pay themselves. This is where the real wages break-out is occurring. Another area of justified alarm is corporate tax avoidance. Business has convinced itself that globalisation means it owes no obligation to society other than to generate profit. When capital took this attitude in the past, either the economic cycle took care of the greed with a recession, or the political system pulled rank. Usually it was both, with the economic crisis prompting the political correction. The global financial crisis has not followed this script, at least to date. If anything, business has become more presumptuous since 2008. Give us a cut in the company tax rate. Fund it with an increase in the GST. There is no economic logic here, only ambit claim.

We are reliving one of the most toxic aspects of the 1970s, when trade unions responded to the global shock of rising inflation by asking for more money, thus killing the jobs of their members. Today it is business which holds the upper hand in the workplace, and it is abusing that privilege at the expense of the wider economy. Every demand for concessions becomes a test of the system, just as with the strikes of the 1970s. This is greed driven by an inferiority complex. Australian firms cannot have much faith in the future if their response to competition from Asia is to ask government for even more power over workers.

Both sides of politics have fallen for the line that in order to maintain our record run of prosperity you have to squeeze the employee, the student, the single parent, the consumer – anyone, really, who does not run a business or own an investment property. It is not unreasonable for politicians to want us to be match-fit for globalisation. But whenever they deliver this message, they do so as an admonition, not a call to arms, and without proposing any clear trade-offs.

Australians are reasonably comfortable with the open economy, provided the government knows whose side it is on. But they don't like change forced on them without explanation, or the buttering-up that follows once government realises it has little support for a policy. Howard rushed WorkChoices through the Senate when he had the balance of power, hoping voters would forget about it by the time of the next election.

They didn't. He eventually apologised, and watered down his legislation so they would be no worse off, but they didn't forgive him.

In a sense, the anxiety about the future begins as a panic of elites. The institutions of politics, media and business remain older, whiter and more masculine than the nation itself. Their response to increased diversity is counterintuitive. The parties know they have to lift their primary vote, news organisations know they have to replenish their ageing audiences, businesses know they have to find new customers. Yet they react to a loss of market share by throwing a tantrum on behalf of what remains of their base, thus reinforcing the loss of market share. When Labor and Liberal politicians ask me why the *Australian* has become so strident in recent years, I remind them that it is behaving no differently to their parties.

Politics is trapped in an old economy mindset while simultaneously advocating for an open economy. Labor wishes collars were still blue, and the Coalition would be happier if Australia could preserve its traditional Anglo identity. Yet income inequality, a diverse but less secure workforce and a rapidly changing ethnic mix are unavoidable features of globalisation. In response, our politicians routinely pick the wrong fights. The contradiction can only be reconciled if we assume the worst: that neither side understands economics as well as it thinks it does. They defer to the market when they should intervene, and they push against our new Eurasian identity when they should embrace it.

Ken Henry says the political system has failed to respond to the challenge of a growing population:

> It's unclear to me to what extent people engaging in policy thinking, including in infrastructure thinking, understand what it is that Australia is facing. What Australia's future really is. I don't want to alarm people with the population projections, but they're out there anyway ... In the second half of the twentieth century, in those five decades, the Australian population increased by between 2.1 million and 2.4 million people [per decade]. In the first decade of this century the Australian population increased by 3 million people. According to the mid-case projections, in each of the next four decades, the Australian population is going to grow by between 3.8 and 4.1 million. That's in each of those decades. Now, I was secretary to the Treasury during pretty much the first decade of this century, and one of the things that was very evident to me was that coping with an increase in the Australian population of 3 million people was more than the Australian policy system could handle.

He says congestion on the roads of Sydney and Melbourne has already reached "unacceptable levels" and is affecting the quality of life in both cities, even as incomes have grown.

> The pressure on urban amenity generally in Sydney in particular, but also to some extent in Melbourne; the pressure being placed on house prices and housing affordability in Sydney and Melbourne and indeed in other cities around the country; the pressure on environmental amenity of new housing sub-divisions being opened up in places where no sane person would ever locate a house, but we're doing it – those sorts of pressures we found ourselves dealing with in the first decade of the twenty-first century, and that was dealing with an increase of 3 million people. There is insufficient comprehension of the magnitude of the task that we confront.

Politicians understand that they need to take infrastructure seriously; their focus groups tell them so. But the very conduct of politics guarantees poor investment decisions, regardless who funds the projects. It is common now for an incoming federal or state government to have a competing wish-list that was drawn up in a political office – and not, as Henry wanted, after a proper market evaluation.

With politics setting the priorities, a change of government inevitably means that existing projects are either cancelled, or slowed to make room in the budget for a new agenda. Once again, it is Victoria which set the benchmark for dysfunction.

Before public transport, the pressing infrastructure need in the state was water security. The Coalition first argued for a desalination plant at the 2006 election, as a response to what had become the worst drought in the state's history. But the Bracks government was not persuaded. It changed its mind after the election, and in 2007 embraced the idea. But then the Coalition turned from champion to opponent. The plant was completed in late 2012 under the new government, but was effectively mothballed early in the new year, with the Coalition water minister reportedly making it his "personal goal" never to order any water from the plant. Imagine Robert Menzies completing Ben Chifley's Snowy Mountain Scheme, then refusing to take any irrigation water or electricity from it. The Victorian pettiness extended to the Metro Rail Project, which was originally identified as a priority in 2008 by an independent report chaired by businessman Rod Eddington. The Coalition government re-evaluated this project along with all others, and in 2014 came up with its own plan, which lapsed with its election defeat that year. In 2015 the new Labor government returned to the original proposal. In those seven years of draft and redraft very little actual work was done.

The federal government has its own interest in interference, because it holds the credit card. And when a government is as overtly political as Tony Abbott's was, the decision to invest is brazenly tribal. Abbott wanted to lock in the Victorian Coalition plan for the East – West Link, and allocated funding before all the contracts had been signed. It suited him to spend the money early, because it made the last federal Labor budget deficit appear larger than it would otherwise have been.

Both sides saw the 2014 state election as a referendum on the project, and when voters threw out the Coalition, the new Labor government assumed that it had won the argument. But Abbott insisted he would only support the Coalition's program, effectively leaving Victoria without any federal funding for public transport in 2015. Meanwhile, Labor had to pay almost a billion dollars in compensation to the consortium that would have built the project under the Coalition. So Victorian taxpayers were short-changed twice, once by the Coalition and once by Labor, all in the name of politics.

At this point in the cycle, when the economy is slowing and federal and state budgets are in deficit, politicians are more risk-averse. They are likely to see congestion back-to-front, as the fault of excessive population growth rather than poor government planning. The populist and the environmentalist can find common cause here: one protests against the influx of migrants, the other fights the apartment towers.

Luckily we have the Bob Carr example to debunk the urban myth that low growth is somehow more sustainable. Let's take the ten years after the *Tampa* and the declaration that Sydney was full, and see what happened. New South Wales Labor mastered politics, and little else. The party machine suffocated the state with its corruption. The dog days for New South Wales were salad days for the rest of the nation. The Australian economy grew by 3.1 per cent on average between 2002 and 2011, from the eve of the mining boom to its end. Every state and territory shared the spoils, except one. New South Wales trailed at just under 2 per cent, far enough behind the rest that the responsibility must rest largely with its government. Nor did low growth make New South Wales more cohesive. While the rest of the nation partied, Sydney exploded with violence across the income spectrum: the white middle class rioted at Cronulla, the white underclass at Macquarie Fields and the black underclass at Redfern.

Demography had the last laugh on Labor. The state that trialled the low-growth option became *more* diverse, as local-born refugees from the Sydney property market moved to Queensland, Western Australia, Victoria and even Tasmania, while a new wave of educated migrants from China and India replaced them. Total population growth slowed, but Sydney became the most cosmopolitan city in the nation.

Today, 39 per cent of Sydney's population are overseas-born, and another 25 per cent have at least one parent who is a migrant. In Perth, the first generation are 37 per cent of the population and the second generation another 25 per cent. In Melbourne, the respective figures are 35 per cent and 24 per cent. The last time migrants accounted for more than a third of the total population of any major settlement was in the 1870s. The reason there is no complacent middle for Australia to aim at is that our continued prosperity is dependent on mass migration. The experiences of Melbourne and Sydney are two sides of the same essential risk. If governments do not plan ahead of that growth, eventually it will overwhelm them.

Australia presently has four world-class cities ranked in the top ten for "liveability" – Melbourne first, Adelaide equal fifth, Sydney seventh and Perth ninth. "Those that score best tend to be mid-sized cities in wealthier countries with a relatively low population density," the *Economist* Intelligence Unit explains. "These can foster a range of recreational activities without leading to high crime levels or overburdened infrastructure."

The evidence from overseas suggests that cities start to become unliveable – that is, gridlocked, polluted and with higher rates of crime and widening gaps between rich and poor – once their population exceeds four or five million. Sydney and Melbourne are approaching that threshold. Australia can only defy the trend if it takes nation-building seriously.

Although Australian governments need to return to pre-deregulation levels of investment in infrastructure, this area of public policy has become too important to leave to politicians. A Reserve Bank – style model is required to identify and rank projects on economic and social grounds, and to recommend timelines for implementation. Politics can then decide which infrastructure to support, and put the case to the public based on independent analysis. Ideally, this system should aim for continuity of investment between governments. If contracts are to be broken, voters should know the cost ahead of an election. The states will need their treasurers to think more like planning ministers; federal treasurers will have to re-educate themselves, and the public, about the value of government borrowing.

Inevitably there will be competition between public and private sectors for investment funds, and for construction workers. The onus is on governments to have projects configured in a way that causes least harm. This should go without saying, but, as we've seen, the conduct of politics often delivers the most perverse results. The key is to think ahead, and for governments to be prepared to dial spending up when the economy is slow, and dial it back down when it is strong. That way, public investment helps to smooth the economic cycle. There is, however, a catch: the federal budget is currently almost as broken as the nation's infrastructure.

THE HOWARD GIFT

Australia did not need to have a decade of budget deficits. We were one of the few rich nations that could profit from the global savings imbalance between China and the United States. Unlike the Americans, we had something the Chinese wanted. One simple contrast shows our advantage. In the ten years from 2005 to 2014, Australia exported $150 billion more to China than it imported – essentially coal and iron going out and computers and large-screen TVs coming in. The Americans accumulated a trade deficit to the Chinese of $2,735 billion over the same period.

Paul Volcker, the celebrated chair of the US Federal Reserve who broke the back of US stagflation in the 1980s, likens the global financial crisis to the earlier Latin American debt crisis. The genesis was the same. A new player entered the global economy with a big bank balance. In the 1970s it was the oil-rich Arab states. "People [were] watching all that money [and asking] how do we recycle it?" he tells me. "Well, they recycled it to Latin America via the big banks. And so there was this big flow of liquidity, which was pleasant when it happened."

The financial institutions thought they were doing Latin American countries a favour by funding their economic development with cheap credit. But it wasn't sustainable. Volcker had a hand in the reckoning. His cure for stagflation was very high interest rates, which hurt the Latin Americans, among others. "But they were going to have a crisis anyway," Volcker says. "It was just a question of time, because they ran out of lenders. Eventually some lender says, 'No, I don't want to lend anymore,' which is what happened in Mexico. So one big lender said that and the others stopped and suddenly you had a crisis where six months earlier everybody was lending like crazy."

> Well, go ahead to the 2000s and you have this big disequilibrium from the United States deficit, from the growing Chinese and Japanese surpluses. But the money flowed and the [deficits] all got financed very easily. What's the worry?
>
> The hardest thing in the world is to take restraining action when things are going very well. You've got no political support for it. They say: 'What are you doing? You're crazy, you know things are going smoothly, let it rip. Don't do anything to disturb the stock market or drive up interest rates or close the budget deficit, we're ok.' It's all very pleasant until something in the chain of financial transactions, which become more and more complex, snaps, and in our case of course it was a subprime mortgage and the mortgage market.

The global financial crisis was a replay of the 1970s, but with three substantial plot twists. First, the money flowed from an emerging economy to the richest nation on earth, which then recycled the money through increasingly dodgy loans. Second, within Europe, the funds travelled from its richest member, Germany, to nations with long histories of victimhood, Greece and Ireland. The third act, which is yet to be written, will be the reckoning for China as it deflates its own credit bubble and shifts its economy away from exports to domestic consumption.

***

A national budget does not necessarily reflect the real economy, but it is a gauge of public values and political temperament. Australia approached the twenty-first century with uncharacteristic prudence. While the Bush administration pushed the US federal budget into deficit to fund massive personal tax cuts, the Howard government took the old-fashioned approach. Income-tax cuts were paid for with a new tax on consumption – the goods and services tax – and Australia's budget remained in surplus. The total tax take was actually a little higher in 2002–03 than it had been in the last year of the old tax system, 1999–2000. It was the ideal fiscal platform from which to greet the rise of China.

In his enthusiasm to sell the GST, John Howard declared that taxpayers would be spared from future bracket creep, the process by which inflation pushes taxpayers up the scales. The worker on average earnings would face a marginal tax rate no higher than 30 cents in the dollar, and no more than 20 per cent of taxpayers would face the top two rates of 42 and 47 cents in the dollar. "You can almost call it the 'bracket creep abolition provision' of the tax plan," he declared, after securing the senate's support for the GST. It was an impossible standard to meet, and as the 2004 election approached, Howard was anxious to adjust the tax scales so that Labor could not accuse him of breaking his promise. That year, I had commissioned research for the *Australian* to show how much tax the government owed workers in bracket creep. By 2005–06, it would be $3.8 billion, if the government did not act. In the 2004 budget Peter Costello obliged with a tax cut worth $3.8 billion by 2005–06. He made a point of underlining the figure when he talked to a huddle of *Australian* reporters at the media lock-up for the budget. The policy nerd in me was chuffed to have got the number right.

If this process had been repeated every few years, no lasting harm would have been done to the budget. But just as these tax cuts landed, the budget also began to catch the first of the revenue windfalls from China. The nation's finances suddenly assumed the character of a magic pudding, as tax collections from companies and investors soared to unprecedented levels. Each time the forecasts were updated, the surplus was larger than expected, even after the tax cuts. At subsequent lock-ups Costello would tell us that some households couldn't have their taxes cut any further, so new payments had to be invented for them, so they wouldn't miss out on the next round.

At each budget from 2005 to 2007, the tax cuts went well beyond bracket creep, and they were not offset by savings from elsewhere. The government assumed the China-led surge in revenue was permanent, and the additional income raised from companies and investors could be returned to workers without risking the bottom line. The total tax take didn't change in this period, but the personal tax burden was now at its lowest level since the 1970s, and it still had further to fall, because Howard had one final tax cut to announce at the 2007 election.

It was too good to be true, of course. Once the global financial crisis struck, the taxes paid by companies and investors collapsed. Of itself, this was not unusual. As boom turns to bust, businesses and their shareholders are more likely to report losses, not profits, on their tax returns. But the personal tax cuts relied on elevated levels of company tax and capital gains tax. Once those props were removed, the budget imploded.

In the Whitlam and Fraser recessions, budget revenue maintained its share of GDP because of bracket creep. In Keating's recession, revenue did drop sharply, but then it recovered with the economy. Again, bracket creep was the key.

This time, revenue fell further, despite low unemployment, and did not bounce back, despite there being no recession. Treasurers on both sides of politics struggled to explain why. Here is Wayne Swan, in his 2013 budget speech: "While our economy remains resilient, powerful global forces and the stubbornly high Australian dollar have savaged budget revenues."

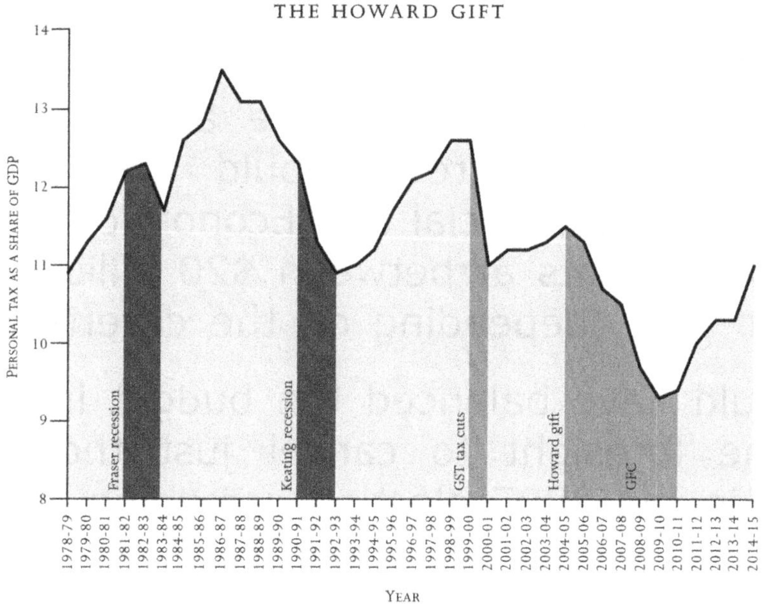

And Joe Hockey in 2015: "In the past twelve months we have coped well with weaker than expected global demand, lower commodity prices and falling revenue. Even in the face of the largest fall in our terms of trade in half a century, which has contributed to a significant fall in tax receipts, our economic plan has helped Australia to have one of the fastest growing economies in the developed world."

These were distractions. The truth is that the problem was homegrown. The decade-long run of personal tax cuts removed the budget's automatic repair mechanism: bracket creep. This is why revenue contracted so sharply, even though the economy was still growing.

In an ideal world, workers who had kept their jobs through a downturn and those who had taken jobs in a recovery would pay more as inflation pushed them up the income-tax scales, until the point where surplus is restored. Only then should tax cuts be considered. Instead Howard and Rudd gave all taxpayers much more than bracket creep would have taken. The National Centre for Social and Economic Modelling put the excess tax cuts at between $20 billion and $31.5 billion per year (depending on the criteria used).

Labor would have balanced the budget in 2012–13 if it had the foresight to cancel just those tax cuts promised in the 2007 election campaign. The political opportunity to do so presented itself during the global financial crisis. The government could have sold the two stimulus payments as a more responsible version of the tax cuts – a larger upfront benefit which did not damage the structure of the budget. But the option was never seriously considered, because Rudd was determined to keep all his promises, to the letter. Even if it had been, the fiscal reward would have been temporary. The hole in the budget was deeper than just one round of unfunded tax cuts and the deficit would have returned in the following year.

Australia does not have a budget crisis, not in the American or European sense of the term. Our taxes and spending remain at the modest end of the spectrum compared to other rich nations. But we have failed to live up to our own previous high standard of prudence.

Ken Henry says that it was not apparent during the mining boom that the tax cuts would be unsustainable, because the budget surplus would always end up higher than forecast. "If you knew for a fact that the revenue surge was going to be temporary, then the smartest thing to do, in fact the only sensible thing to do really, would be to bank the lot of it, put it in the sovereign wealth fund. No question about it." But Henry and his colleagues thought at least some of the extra revenue was permanent, and so it could be safely given back to workers. With hindsight, he says there were two parts of the revenue surge that were not permanent: capital gains, which is counted under personal income tax; and company tax.

> So should we have known that? It is certainly arguable that we should have known it. But every time the government put out a budget or a budget update from 2003–04 through to 2007–08, the government had to admit to the Australian population that revenue was much, much more buoyant than what they'd been saying it was. Even though they were providing big income tax cuts and increases in family payments along the way. Very difficult in that environment to firstly convince yourself that it's only temporary and then, if you have convinced yourself, you've got to turn around and convince everybody else in

> the room that what appears to be happening is not actually happening.

John Howard and Peter Costello did not consciously set out to make the income-tax system an agent for inequality. They thought the reverse would occur: by reducing the burden on the top, everyone would want to climb the ladder. No one doubted the theory in the government or the bureaucracy. Tax cuts were supposed to reward effort, and to encourage people to save and invest.

Costello lifted the threshold to the point where only 2 per cent of taxpayers paid the top rate by 2007–08. This is what made the tax system less progressive. Many higher income earners suddenly found they were paying the marginal tax rate of 30 cent that was meant for average earners.

If the tax cuts had encouraged Australia to work harder, economists could say they were worth the trouble. But productivity stalled during this period, which begs the question whether all that money made us soft. One thing is clear, though: the tax cuts made Australia less fair.

We know this now because of a fascinating study undertaken by Nicolas Herault and Francisco Azpitarte for the Brotherhood of St Laurence and the Melbourne Institute of Applied Economic and Social Research. They looked at the period of our greatest prosperity, from the late 1990s to the eve of the global financial crisis, and found that, measured in take-home pay, inequality increased. The Howard government tax cuts were not the only reason, but they were a significant factor. "We find that the direct effect of tax-transfer policy reforms accounts for approximately half of the observed increase in income inequality over this period," they wrote.

This is the part of the Great Recession we did not avoid. We had imported the American disease of budget-busting tax cuts for the rich. The point here is that rising inequality is not always the result of market failure: it may also be due to government failure. It is true that politicians no longer have an influence on wages beyond the minimum rate. The open model effectively sets the market rate. But politicians still influence disposable income through the tax and payments system. That will never change, and nor should it in a democracy.

What is striking in retrospect is that Treasury, and the governments of Howard, Rudd, Gillard and Abbott, convinced themselves that the budget was basically out of their hands. Not even the global financial crisis changed that thinking. The emergency was deemed to be temporary. The government should only provide stimulus for a year or two – after that, the budget was supposed to go back into neutral gear, neither slowing nor speeding up the economy.

By degrees, the Coalition and Labor convinced themselves that they were absolved of responsibility for the mood swings of a China-dominated global economy. The revenue windfall could be given away, and when it disappeared the deficit could blamed on the rest of the world.

The Howard Gift was not easily retrieved, because the economy remained sluggish after the global financial crisis. Any repair to the revenue side of the budget had to be offset with compensation to ensure that households continued to spend and businesses continued to hire. The Gillard government followed this risk-averse script by giving back more than it collected from the carbon and mining taxes.

With the personal tax scales considered off-limits, Labor looked to the spending side of the budget and, in doing so, reinforced the unfairness of the Howard Gift. The burden of expenditure cuts fell on the most vulnerable members of the community. The most callous of those measures was the Gillard government's decision to slash the benefits of single mothers. The policy was supposed to encourage them to move from welfare to work, but it did not achieve its goal because unemployment was rising at the time. In the end, thousands of single mothers had their disposable income reduced by more than $100 per week and for no good cause, because the budget was still in deficit.

It was Labor's misfortune to be on the other side of the revenue boom – the bust. Every time the budget was updated, the deficit blew out. But Labor had already spent the forecast revenue before it was received, repeating the Coalition's mistake of assuming the windfalls would be permanent.

John Howard remains unrepentant. You'd expect nothing less. He is like Keating with the recession. These were the tax cuts we had to have, and he presents them in the same way as a profitable company might a Christmas bonus for its workforce, or a dividend for its shareholders. "There is a thing called the money belonging to the public and if the country is doing well, why can't the taxpayer have some of that money back," he says. "That was our view – and it was a view right across the government. I mean, there may have been individual arguments about the extent of this or that decision, but there was no serious dispute, I can tell you, inside the government about the desirability of giving tax cuts. And I don't also remember tremendous resistance from within the bureaucracy about the idea of giving tax cuts. There seemed to be a general acceptance. You provide for defence; you provide for the essentials for the not-so-well-off; you provide for the Future Fund; you have a surplus of at least 1 per cent of GDP; and the rest, frankly, should be given back in tax cuts."

Leave to one side for now the question of whether that money should have been reinvested in infrastructure, or used to provide better government services, and ponder what the taxpayers did when they got their money back. They spent most of it, of course. But they wanted something else, and threw out the government despite its apparent generosity. It was clear by 2006 that the tax cuts were not helping the government in the electorate, but that only made Howard more determined to provide another round of them, and then another.

The Liberal Party pollster and strategist Mark Textor says Howard sacrificed his image as a resolute leader when he went on that spending spree between 2004 and 2007. "It was lazy money," he says. The public reaction was, "'Ok, anyone can throw money at things and frankly if I want a government to throw money at things, Labor does that better than the Liberals. So if it's really now about throwing money at things, I'll vote Labor.'"

There were other, more important reasons why Howard lost office in 2007. His breach of faith on WorkChoices was the most decisive issue.

"They saw him being opportunistic," Textor explains, "taking the opportunity that a majority in the lower and the upper house presented to sneak in a set of reforms for which there was no mandate and they thought, 'What's this about? I don't see the national good in this [and] I'm a little bit suspicious about why it was introduced.'"

But the cost of neglecting fiscal policy is the big lesson to be drawn from this era. Howard changed the budget from being a document primarily concerned with the economy to one with a purpose that was overtly political. He taught people to expect a handout outside an election campaign, which created a permanent sense of entitlement. The targeting was so obvious that the media could almost guess which section of the community would be next in line. His successors fell into the same habit, even though the budget was in deficit. Kevin Rudd increased the age pension in the 2009 budget after grey voters complained they had missed out the year before. Tony Abbott tried to buy the women's vote with a paid parental leave scheme that even Howard thought was too generous.

With each futile attempt to bribe, government wasted another opportunity to reconsider the role of the budget in the twenty-first century. The public has had the more economically rational view on this issue for some time now. They want the government to stop throwing money at them and spend it instead on infrastructure. Although the first phase of the mining boom was the time to make those investments, it is still possible to do so with the budget in deficit. The key is to borrow while global interest rates remain at their lowest levels in about 500 years. Surely our federal and state governments can identify projects that generate a return to the economy above the cost of the loan. The budget need not blow out. Only the interest bill from new loans is counted in the bottom line, and that cost could be funded with a small tax rise, perhaps an increase in the Medicare levy.

There would be understandable political queasiness about taking such a step. Debt has been a dirty word since the Whitlam and Fraser deficits. But Australia remains an anomaly of globalisation: a nation that can afford to borrow more. The federal government debt, which is the sum of the budget deficits since 2008, is expected to peak at 18 per cent of gross domestic product this year, before falling. In Europe, government debts of 100 per cent or more of GDP are commonplace.

The obvious danger is that politics uses infrastructure as an excuse to leave the budget in deficit. Yet the borrowing would be more credible to the electorate, and to the financial markets, if the budget was returned to surplus. It would, in fact, signal a new form of discipline, as governments moved from vote-buying to nation-building.

***

In all of this, neither side has been prepared to confront the structure of the budget. They crab-walk around the revenue side of the problem, and take indiscriminate nips at the spending side.

The first budget after the global financial crisis forecast a recession for Australia, with unemployment peaking at more than 8 per cent. When the recession did not come, Treasury told the government that a small surplus could be achieved in 2012–13. Wayne Swan stuck to that deadline in his next three budgets, thus elevating a forecast into an iron-clad commitment. When he finally gave up the quest at the end of 2012, the goal of surplus had been pushed back to 2015–16. So much political pain could have been avoided if Treasury had stuck to its original pessimistic forecast.

If Tony Abbott and Joe Hockey had been doing their sums in opposition, they might have encouraged Labor to cut harder and to broaden the tax base, so that they would inherit a budget on the right trajectory. But they were having too much fun shouting down every Labor proposal to tighten the budget. That's politics, perhaps, and they'd happily plead guilty to the charge of pulling down the government. But they also promised to fix the budget with a formula that never made sense given the deficit they knew they would inherit. Abbott, in particular, somehow thought he could charm the budget into surplus while reducing taxes and increasing spending.

Joe Hockey's first budget, in 2014, pushed back a surplus to 2018–19. In the following year, he said we would have to wait till 2019–20. At the mid-year update last December, the new treasurer, Scott Morrison, placed his opening bid for surplus at 2020–21.

The most telling article written after Abbott's demise was by Dennis Atkins of the *Courier-Mail.* It revealed a proposal put to cabinet, a fortnight before Abbott's dismissal, to scrap one of his government's own taxes. Originally a Labor idea, the $500 million deposit levy on the banks was a form of insurance in case one of them needed to be bailed out in the future. The measure had been announced in Hockey's second budget, and was due to take effect in January 2016.

"Hockey, who was desperate to get as much money as he could to drive down the deficit, wanted that $500 million but Abbott saw it as an easy way to attack Labor's Bill Shorten," Atkins wrote.

One of the leading opponents of scrapping the tax at that meeting was Malcolm Turnbull, who said it was simply an insurance levy such as many businesses incur when dealing with large amounts of money.

Abbott brushed off these objections, saying it was a good way to brand Shorten as a "bank bandit" who always looked to raising taxes.

Turnbull later told colleagues the government had "thrown away half a billion a year for a press release." Abbott was certainly not the first prime minister to see the budget as a plaything of politics. But it was unusual to attack your own deficit-reduction measure for the sake of a slogan. In Abbott's binary view of the budget, taxes were evil and government defined itself by the voters it gave money to.

If Turnbull is to reset the budget debate, he has to abandon the Liberal mantra that taxes must always be cut. Both sides of the budget have to be deployed in the search for fairness and efficiency, and in the present climate that means an active search for ways to unwind the Howard Gift without crashing the economy. The most obvious target for Turnbull is the tax concessions for superannuation. There is no economic case for government continuing to subsidise the retirement savings of higher-income earners while providing virtually no support at all for lower-income earners. This part of the Howard Gift has to be taken back before the next global shock, when the budget will be called on to stimulate the economy again.

A RECESSION WE HAVE TO HAVE?

It's time for a refresher course on the meaning of recession, because Australia has entered the danger zone where history warns that one is coming. Two threats in particular are coalescing, one local and one international. The property market is overheated in Sydney, and to a lesser extent in Melbourne. And the global economy is facing its third serious downturn in nine years. Our open economic model has shown it can cope with either one of these risks, but we don't know if it can handle both together.

The past offers little comfort, because the moments of Australia's greatest economic vulnerability come when soaring house prices combine with a global shock. If the worst comes to pass this year and China joins the United States and Europe as victims of capitalism's extended crisis, a recession of some kind will be difficult to avoid.

The housing bubble is the economist's version of Gallipoli, a nation-scarring event which destroys a generation. Our first global humiliation had its source in the Melbourne and Sydney land busts of the 1890s, which ended our long colonial reign as the world's richest people. Property prices collapsed by 50 per cent and 25 per cent respectively, banks closed their doors and unemployment jumped to double digits and remained there for a decade. The Australian economy took twenty years to recover the loss of income from that depression. The Keating recession of 1990–91 contained every one of those failures: a housing boom and bust; the failure of state banks, building societies and credit unions; and unemployment remaining above 10 per cent for a number of years. Property prices didn't fall by as much, but they did stagnate for the remainder of the 1990s.

Although the IMF thinks our economy will keep growing, it sees property as the biggest domestic threat: "A sharp correction in house prices, possibly driven by Sydney, could be triggered by external conditions ... or a domestic shock to employment. This might have wider ramifications if it affects confidence."

Furthermore, "Over half of Australia's exports go to emerging Asia and nearly two thirds are non-rural commodity exports. An unexpectedly sharp fall in iron ore prices could reduce prices below production costs, and further dent incomes and growth. It would also likely dent foreign investment in Australian property and other markets, adversely affecting prices."

Hooked on capital gain and reliant on the trade of one big country: this is the familiar face of Australian smugness. But it is more than that. This particular housing boom, which began in 2012, defies the old rule that prices only climb at times of reckless confidence in the future. The economy has been soft, and our politics dysfunctional. Neither would seem to warrant another splurge on housing. Yet our two most globalised cities are behaving as if the party will never stop. The explanation is not merely economic, but cultural. Australians now see property as a shield against globalisation. Fear, not greed, has been driving up prices. This is an unprecedented development, which is drawing us ever closer to the crisis we thought we had side-stepped in 2008–09.

The Reserve Bank has been powerless to stop this latest spike in property prices because interest rates no longer work the way the open economic model intended. To understand why, it is worth recalling the last occasion that Sydney menaced the national economy. It was the giddy period between 2001 and 2003, when politics and the media competed to talk up the property market. John Howard had doubled the first home owner's grant, *Kath & Kim* hit our television screens, and households were spending more in total than they earned.

"I thought we were very close to having a bubble," the bank's governor at the time, Ian Macfarlane, says. "We had house prices going up by 20 per cent per annum; we had lending for housing going up by 20-plus per cent per annum. We had nearly half of it going into speculative investment housing. We had all these spruikers going around telling you how to get rich quick and, as someone pointed out to me ... we had something like seven programs on prime-time television telling you how to get rich quick through property development. So you put all those things together [and] it sounds like you're getting very close to a bubble."

Sydney house prices had run so far ahead of the rest of the nation that by the end of 2003 they were 40 per cent above Melbourne's and Brisbane's and 50 per cent above Perth's.

Macfarlane says: "We put a lot of thought into understanding what was happening and what we saw we didn't like very much. Fortunately, we had other reasons as well to raise interest rates. So we raised interest rates twice in 2002 and again twice in 2003."

In the end, house prices didn't collapse. "If they had've collapsed, that would have proved that it was a bubble. But they flattened right out, and there was very little growth for the next two or three years. In fact, in Sydney they fell, because Sydney was the hottest market. We got through that, I think, in reasonable shape, although we're always going to be worried from time to time about house prices in Australia. It's part of the landscape."

Howard wasn't happy. As he approached the 2004 election, he found voters concerned about interest rates. He framed the campaign as a question of trust: who would you trust to keep rates low, him or Mark Latham? And he began showering voters with cash. The baby bonus and a record boost to family payments were the down-payment. After the election, the money kept pouring onto the kitchen table. As mentioned, each budget of Howard's final term contained a tax cut larger than its predecessor's. Once again, the Reserve Bank was able to reduce the risk of inflation by countering the tax cuts with higher interest rates.

An unintended benefit of this was that Australia had a larger buffer than other rich nations when the global financial crisis hit. Rates could therefore be cut often and quickly to restore consumer and business confidence. The US Federal Reserve, by contrast, had slashed interest rates before the financial meltdown of September 2008. By Christmas, the US official rate was zero and it would remain there for the next seven years.

Another advantage not widely appreciated at the time was that Sydney did not get ahead of itself during the first or second phases of the mining boom. House prices were essentially flat between 2004 and 2011, which meant the city most likely to import the contagion of speculation that infected the US and European property markets did no harm. With Sydney in remission, the banks were able to take their business to the rest of the country. Melbourne and Perth prices came within 10 per cent of Sydney's, and Brisbane within 20 per cent. Although housing was now less affordable across the continent, the important thing was that prices did not overshoot because the Reserve Bank was able to keep lifting interest rates throughout the boom. Also, our banks were well regulated and, unlike their counterparts in the United States, did not lend recklessly. The open model was at its best in those years.

Soon after the emergency cuts of the global financial crisis, the Reserve Bank wanted to raise interest rates to more normal levels, and for a while it seemed it would have its way, because we were riding the back-to-back recovery waves of the Rudd - Gillard stimulus program and the second mining boom. But then interest rates had to be slashed again, as the eye of capitalism's storm reached Europe and the mining boom peaked. This was the period when the open model lost its flexibility. Australian interest rates were cut ten times between November 2011 and May 2015, to a new record low of 2 per cent.

Inevitably, these reductions awakened the demon of the Sydney property market. House prices in Sydney have jumped by 15 per cent each year since 2011. Apartment prices have risen by 11 per cent. In Melbourne, the annual rises have been 6 per cent for houses and 3 per cent for apartments. The Reserve Bank could not respond with higher interest rates as it did before, because the rest of the economy was weak. Victoria, Queensland and South Australia have each been close to recession on a couple of occasions since 2011. Western Australia is coming off the high of the mining boom, while Tasmania has already suffered a recession.

Without the interest-rate lever to pull, authorities have encouraged banks to restrict lending to investors. But this is a second-best option. Sydney is almost back where it was in 2003, a third more expensive than Melbourne and 40 per cent more expensive than Perth and Brisbane. The IMF says Sydney is one of the most expensive markets in the world and Australian housing is overvalued by about 10 per cent. If prices were to fall even by half that amount, it could be the psychological trigger for a recession. The Reserve Bank has left itself just enough room to reduce interest rates again in the event of another crisis. But it can't go much lower before we join the rest of the world in the quicksand of a zero official interest rate, from which no rich nation has yet been able to launch a sustainable recovery.

THE RISE, FALL AND RISE OF THE SYDNEY PROPERTY MARKET

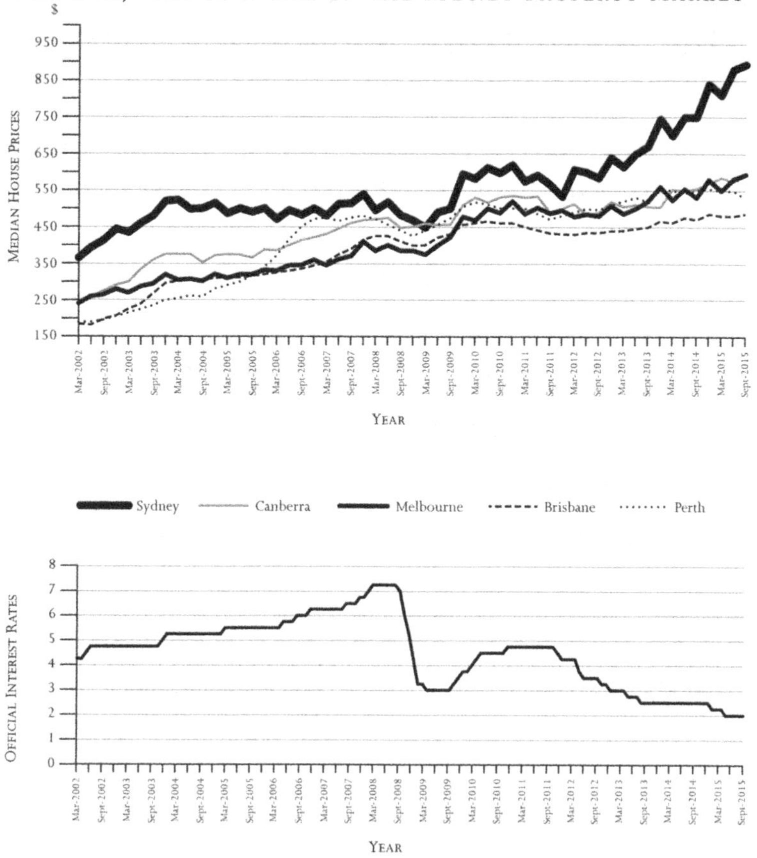

On top of the list of national regrets if we do fall into recession this year or next will be the role that politics played in fostering our property obsession. Every prime minister and treasurer since Hawke and Keating has indulged it with tax concessions. Keating did try to include housing in his program to modernise the economy. When he abolished negative gearing for investment properties in 1985, he said it was "an outrageous rort" which was holding back investment in more productive areas of the economy.

The outrageous rort was restored two years later, and for the simplest political reason. The Sydney property market had cooled, and Keating wanted to revive it ahead of the NSW state election in 1988. He didn't save the Labor government, but he did bring the speculators back, and prices have been edging further out of reach of first-time buyers ever since.

The landlord class in Australia – the number of people owning more than one property – numbered 600,000 in 1998–99. A decade later, their ranks had doubled to 1.275 million, or almost 13 per cent of individuals. John Howard gave the investor another leg up by halving the capital gains tax rate in 1999. That was the last year our landlord class declared a profit. Between 2000–01 and 2012–13, the most recent year for which statistics are available, our landlord class lost $66.3 billion, or $5.1 billion per year, more than they made in rental income. I'm pulling your leg. They didn't lose this money. Their fellow taxpayers did, because the landlords wrote off the losses against other income, thereby reducing the total tax they paid.

On the latest count, Australia has 1.9 million property investors, comprising 15 per cent of all taxpayers. They prefer to invest in existing properties, thus inflating prices without adding to the stock of housing. In any normal market, higher prices would encourage new entrants to increase the supply. But property is the blind spot of the open model – a corrupted market created with the blessing of politics.

This time-bomb is not easily defused. The best opportunity to curtail negative gearing was during the global financial crisis, but the Rudd government did not seriously consider it. Only now, in Opposition, is Labor prepared to address the mistake Keating made three decades ago. It wants to abolish negative gearing from 2017 for those who buy existing properties. The policy, announced in February, should encourage the Turnbull government to do something similar in the May budget. Let's assume the best of politics for a change, and trust that the parties will agree to remove the tax incentives for speculation in bricks and mortar. The question is whether it is already too late to reduce the threat of a bust.

One of the most concerning aspects of the housing boom since 2011 is the resumption of the debt cycle. Australian households owe more now than they did before the global financial crisis. Let that thought sink in. Record low interest rates did not encourage us to repay existing loans quicker. After a few years of belt-tightening, we returned to the bad habits of the Howard era.

Household debt peaked at 172 per cent of disposable income in mid-2007. By the end of 2011, it had been reduced to 167 per cent, still high by world standards but pointing in the right direction – down. The latest figure is 185 per cent. More than half the increase of the past four years is explained by the landlord class. If there is a recession, this is the group that will be kicking itself for borrowing too much.

Even if we stage another great escape and the economy keeps growing into the next decade, the open model has demonstrated its limitations. The inability to contain the Sydney property market reminds us that interest rates are an inherently blunt weapon. They can't control a boom once it is underway.

***

Recessions are notoriously tricky to predict, and even harder to define. Politicians and the media rely on the formula coined by Paul Keating in 1990: an economy that contracts for two quarters in a row. It is an arbitrary standard. For example, GDP could fall by 0.1 per cent and 0.1 per cent in consecutive quarters and that would be a recession. But if it collapsed by 1 per cent in one quarter and grew by 0.1 per cent the next, presumably it wasn't.

"If the Australian economy has a couple of quarters of negative growth, where instead of growing by three quarters of a percentage point it goes backward by 0.1 or something, does that really matter?" Ken Henry asks. "Politically that matters a lot. But does it really matter? Well, it probably doesn't matter a hell of a lot to Australia. But if it's a recession that gives us 10 per cent unemployment, then we really should be worried. We should do whatever we can to avoid that. [More than half] the people aged over forty-five who lost their jobs in the early 1990s recession never worked a day again in their lives. That is a consequence that should be avoided not at any cost, but at any reasonable cost."

The unemployment rate is the key to distinguishing the deep recessions from the shallow ones. Once it starts climbing, it is already too late to prevent a hard landing. The Keating recession cast a shadow over the entire 1990s and it wasn't until 2003 that the unemployment rate returned to its pre-recessionary low.

The reason the rest of the world still envies us is that our unemployment rate was contained during the global financial crisis. It did not cross 6 per cent during the crisis, which meant it could be quickly brought back below 5 per cent in the recovery.

As the economist John Quiggin pointed out, the initial success of the Rudd government's stimulus program meant Australia also avoided the next trap in the crisis, "the swing to extreme austerity that characterised most of the developed world."

> Even Abbott and Hockey, despite talking up a debt and deficit crisis, shied away from really serious austerity measures. The results speak for themselves, particularly in the job market. Australia's employment–population ratio was barely affected by the global financial crisis. In Britain, the United States, Ireland and Canada, employment fell sharply ... and has never recovered.

But our unemployment rate has been drifting higher since mid-2011, and almost every economic advantage we enjoyed before the global financial crisis has either diminished or disappeared. The interest-rate buffer is almost gone; the budget is in deficit; households are deeper in debt; house prices are inflated; and China cannot come to the rescue again.

The next global shock, whenever it comes, will find us with our economic guard down, and a political system that has shredded its authority.

RECONSTRUCTION

Any system, be it political, economic or environmental, must adapt to maintain stability. Otherwise, the system risks collapse. In the past, Australian complacency would be broken by an economic crisis, which would trigger a political crisis. Stability would only be restored after politics designed a new economic model. The cycles of recession and renewal have been inverted in the twenty-first century, with a political crisis preceding an economic crisis. It has been twenty-five years since our last deep recession, yet in the past five years we have had as many prime ministers as Greece.

Politics has brought this crisis on itself by underestimating the public. Mark Textor says voters have grasped the meaning of the open model and are ruthlessly applying its lessons at the ballot box.

> Before the '80s, government guaranteed a lot of things. They guaranteed a pension for life, they guaranteed certain Australian industries. People understood that was changing, but they also understood that when that changed they should guarantee less [in return]. If you want me to live in an economy where I can trade and work with whoever I want – if you are offering me less loyalty as a government – I can offer you less loyalty as a voter.

Australians fired their first warning shot at the 1990 election, when they gave the main parties their lowest combined primary vote in almost fifty years. Support for the minor parties was 17.4 per cent, and Labor became the first government to be re-elected with a primary vote below 40 per cent.

It was a harbinger. At the *Tampa* election of 2001, the hung parliament of 2010 and Tony Abbott's victory in 2013, the minor-party vote was even higher than in 1990. The last election was the most fractured of all, with voters damning both sides. Labor suffered its lowest primary vote since the Great Depression, while the Coalition's primary was the lowest for an incoming conservative government in Australian history. The structural decline in the base vote of the main parties has undermined the policymaking process. Governments live in dread of losing power after a single term, and so they churn through announcements in a pitiful search for approval in the polls. Oppositions understand the fear of the incumbent, because they lived with it only a few years earlier. They obstruct because they know it's the simplest way back into office. Politics has casualised its own employment market, making every position in the system temporary.

Malcom Turnbull had almost six years in the wilderness to observe both our domestic political crisis and the global economic crisis. The time between losing the Opposition leadership in December 2009 and seizing the prime ministership last September is the political equivalent of an older worker retraining for a new career. Both sides of politics have compelling redemption stories to encourage Turnbull, in which broken or divisive men used their second chance to change the country and restore confidence in the system. John Curtin and Bob Hawke gave up the grog before Labor could trust them with the leadership. Robert Menzies and John Howard came back as conservative leaders who could relate to the people. The catch for Turnbull is that he has to be both Curtin and Menzies, and Hawke and Howard, to succeed. He has to author a new model *and* run a long-term government.

It is telling that Turnbull sought the prime ministership with a call for nation-building and innovation that echoed Kevin Rudd's campaign against John Howard in 2007. Will he run with the baton of active government, or lose direction and ultimately drop it, as Rudd did after the global financial crisis?

Turnbull's first six months as prime minister have not been encouraging. If he had a new model, we should be able to recite it by now. Instead, we witnessed an aimless debate on the GST. What has been missing so far is an explanation of the economic problems Turnbull wants to solve. He can't do this until he removes the blinkers of ideology and nostalgia from his side of politics in the way Curtin and Hawke once did for Labor.

The Coalition can't lay claim to the future until it adjusts to the two big shocks of our age. The first shock is that the version of capitalism favoured by conservatives is broken. The crisis entered its ninth year in 2016, which places it in the same category as the global depressions of the 1890s and 1930s. The epicentre has shifted from the American housing market and Wall Street to Europe. Now it threatens China, the nation most likely to end Australia's long economic winning streak. The crisis won't pass until capitalism finds a new source of market-based growth. Until then, as the IMF and others have been saying for some years, governments must step in to fill the void. Not as temporary support for their economies, but to fix the things that are holding back recovery, most notably public infrastructure. Turnbull is to the right of most Australians on economics, and a little to their left on social policy. He has faith in markets and multiculturalism. However, fate has dealt him the responsibility of renewing the open model by going against his own instincts for smaller government.

The second shock is that the international community may finally be ready to tackle climate change. This should be Turnbull's vindication: the times finally suit the call he made in 2009 for a market-based response. But the price he paid for removing Tony Abbott was the retention of the former prime minister's compromised policy, which relies on government spending to reduce greenhouse-gas emissions. It cannot work without tearing an even larger hole in the budget. In its first full year of operation, 2014–15, Direct Action saw emissions rise, reversing gains made under Labor's carbon tax.

Perhaps Turnbull is waiting for an election win before he reveals a new model. But events may overwhelm him. No post-war government has increased its majority in its second term, so Turnbull could conceivably be governing on a parliamentary knife-edge. And then there is the ever-present danger of another economic setback.

***

Most high-income nations would still love to have our problems. Australia is one of the few advanced economies with demography on its side. We have not yet hit the speed hump of ageing. Our open economic model remains the gold standard. But politics is killing our future because the open model can't manage the transition anymore. The Sydney property market has seen to that. The open model was supposed to ensure stability by removing four key prices in the economy from political control: the currency, interest rates, tariffs and wages. The job of steering the economy passed from government to the invisible hand of the market. If the economy went off-course, the Reserve Bank was there to guide it back to safer waters. Governments forgot that markets and central banks can fail just as spectacularly as interventionist politicians.

Australia remains unnecessarily exposed to the extended crisis in capitalism because our leaders stopped thinking. They behave as if a better system will fall out of the sky and relieve us of the responsibility of making our own future.

Today the world has no better system for us to choose, because every version of capitalism is under attack. The United States, Europe and China account for more than half the world's total production. Each has a readily identifiable model. The Americans have the freest markets, the Europeans the most comprehensive welfare system, and the Chinese the most active government sector. None can say their particular phase of the crisis is behind them. None can point to a better model. They serve only as warnings for Australia of the policies that don't work.

The disruptions we associate with the twenty-first century have a long tail winding back to the 1980s. They are an inescapable part of globalisation, generating income and instability in almost equal measure. The United States carried the global economy in the 1980s and '90s, even as its innovations in finance and technology undermined it. China has been underwriting it since 2007, even though its savings glut helped precipitate the global financial crisis. Within Europe, Germany serves the same conflicting role as growth engine and unforgiving banker.

The shifts in global economic power are more nuanced than the easy headline of Asia rising at the expense of the North Atlantic. The first fifteen years of the Asian century have witnessed a boom and a bust in Europe, a long stagnation in the United States, and the extraordinary growth in China cancelling an almost equivalent loss in Japan. Europe, not China, accounted for the largest share of global growth between 2000 and 2007 and almost caught the United States in total size before it was overwhelmed by the global financial crisis.

China has been responsible for just over a third of total world growth over the past seven years, a position that is no longer sustainable. By 2014, the United States accounted for 22.5 per cent of the global economy, the Euro area was a much diminished 17.4 per cent, while China reached 13.4 per cent. The test of the Chinese model is whether it consolidates those gains, or suffers a severe correction like the Europeans.

Intriguingly, China's share of the global economy today is almost identical to Japan's at the turn of the century. Japan was fading long before the Asian century for reasons that should terrify the Europeans today, and perhaps even the Chinese. Japan's financial system never recovered from its property bubble in the late 1980s, and now, as its population ages, new sources of dynamism are hard to find. The Chinese appreciate this danger, and have taken steps to inspire a new baby boom by abandoning their one-child policy. But the conundrum has not changed: will they grow old before they become rich?

The sequencing of the crisis, from the United States to Europe and now China, suggests that the American economy will drive global growth in the next few years. Remarkably, if it does, it will be as a damaged society, unrecognisable from its former arrogant self, which swaggered through the 1980s and '90s chanting "U.S.A, U.S.A."

The young working men and women of the Reagan era have reached middle age and they are not coping with change. A troubling spike in deaths by drug poisoning, suicide and chronic liver disease has increased the mortality rate for those aged forty-five to fifty-four. This is unusual in a high-income society, and a vivid illustration of the human cost of a free-market society without an adequate safety net. Research by Princeton University's Anne Case and Angus Deaton compared midlife mortality rates between 1999 and 2013 in the United States and six other rich nations, including Australia. Only the US showed an increase in deaths per 100,000 people, an extraordinary finding on its own. But when Case and Deaton broke down mortality rates among white, black and Hispanic Americans, they found only white Americans were affected by this scourge. (Mortality rates fell sharply for both black and Hispanic Americans.) The researchers said "the epidemic of pain, suicide, and drug overdoses" may be tied to loss of economic security and widening income inequality since the 1970s. "Many of the baby-boom generation are the first to find, in midlife, that they will not be better off than were their parents. Growth in real median earnings has been slow for this group, especially those with only a high school education."

Politicians here might shrug and say that this doesn't apply to Australia, because we recorded the second-lowest death rate for middle-aged men and women after Sweden. We don't have the American problem of a white underclass. But we do have a prosperity gap between new Australians and the local-born. The post-war assumption that migrants to Australia will only do the work that the locals don't want no longer applies. Now migrants are also being hired for work that the locals are not qualified for.

Professor Bob Gregory has found that migrants account for virtually all the full-time jobs created in Australia since 2007. They didn't displace the local-born; they just took the cream of the new positions on offer, most notably in the professions. Our "extraordinary economic success since the global financial crisis owes a great deal to the increased level of national income" generated by these latest arrivals, Gregory concluded. "Mining booms come and go, but large population changes last forever."

On the other hand, the success of the migrant raises the risk of a local backlash, and the possibility that one of our main parties will take a detour down the American road of bigotry. If the political system couldn't cope with the infrastructure demands of the past decade, how will it respond to a future in which a fraction of the local-born feel that they have been pushed to the margins of society? The logical answer is to dramatically increase public investment in education to ensure these local-born are not left behind. But this would require a change of mindset in the Coalition, which supports private systems over public, and the winners of deregulation over the losers.

The onus is on Malcom Turnbull to repair the social contract before inequality becomes entrenched. He does seem to understand this need. He said he wants Australia to remain a high-wage society with a generous social safety net. Yet something doesn't add up. He also presents as a leader who wants to cut taxes further and shrink the size of government. The experience of the twenty-first century so far tells us these ideas are not compatible.

The tax cuts of the boom years, which favoured higher income earners, and the spending cuts since the global financial crisis, which punished those at the bottom, overturned a century of political tradition to promote egalitarianism through the federal budget. Turnbull can't improve the open model by repeating the formula which alienated the electorate in the first place.

The political dialogue about tax has to change. This is an argument conservatives can make in the twenty-first century if they are prepared to learn from the example of Labor in the 1980s. Hawke and Keating inherited a budget with a spending problem, and badly designed taxes. They cut spending and simplified the tax system, but did not reduce overall revenue. They explained to the public that they were correcting for the spending errors of the Whitlam era, and Labor supporters accepted the argument. Turnbull can do the same on the revenue side by explaining the budget policy mistakes of the Howard era. Too much money was given to those who didn't need it, and too little of it was put aside for the future.

Politicians mistake the trade-offs of deregulation for immutable laws, when in fact they are choices made by politicians, whether actively or by neglect. Deregulation need not have increased household debt to the extent that it has, nor led to a greater concentration of national wealth in the property market. These are not rational outcomes of a free market, but the result of political decisions to favour one form of investment over all others. Governments used financial deregulation to create the illusion of sound economic management. They boasted budget surpluses, while encouraging households to take on debt.

The danger was not sufficiently appreciated during the long credit boom. Economies were strong, and governments could look forward to re-election. Once the global financial crisis hit, households returned to their pre-deregulation levels of thrift. That rational switch from borrower to saver has undermined capitalism ever since, even in Australia, because markets cannot thrive without confident consumers.

Having come through the global financial crisis so well, Australia should have been able to shift some of the risk back onto the government balance sheet without European-style levels of public debt. I know every second politician has screamed about debt and deficit, but this is one of the most necessary steps in the transition. Households will not be assured about the future until they get on top of their own debts, and see the government taking more responsibility in areas such as infrastructure.

To date, the shortcut of populism is more appealing than the intellectual ordeal of adapting the open model for the twenty-first century. Labor had a reasonable expectation of returning to government this year if Tony Abbott was prime minister. If so, it would have been the first federal Labor Opposition to be elected on the basis of a protest vote. Now it is hoping that the loss won't be devastating. The election, and the future, is Malcolm Turnbull's to lose.

The test Turnbull has set for himself, and the community, is to exploit the transition to Australia's advantage. The nation is smarter than its politicians have given it credit for. The workforce already reflects that in the rise of the professional. Turnbull should use his greatest electoral asset – his intelligence – to argue for a smarter nation. While we will never be big enough to play the market-rigging games of the Americans, Chinese or Germans, we do have something they crave: potential. It may be hard to believe after a quarter of a century of uninterrupted growth, but Australia is still developing. We remain an anomaly among high-income nations, a small population in charge of a resource-rich continent. While our natural advantage in coal and iron ore risks turning to curse now that the minerals cycle has turned, we still have a country to which people want to migrate.

The global financial crisis is forcing every nation to re-examine the role of government. High-income nations are investing more in physical infrastructure, education and innovation. They are doing so to prop up their economies in crisis. Australia can intervene from a position of relative strength. What is missing at the moment is genuine political insight. The challenge for government in the twenty-first century is to think for the long term. Planning is the simplest political concept, but it goes against every instinct of the contemporary leader. Part of the problem is that the main parties are stuck in the wrong past: they keep looking to the market to fix problems that can only be solved by government. Both the conservatives and Labor need to give Howard, Keating and Hawke a break and look instead to the post-war reconstruction of Curtin, Chifley and Menzies for inspiration. If Australia is to stay ahead of the pack, it needs governments that understand markets well enough to know where government belongs. Otherwise, Australia will become globalisation's next and most unnecessary victim.

The one thing weighing us down is the chip on our shoulder. In the past, we only found inspiration after the fall. It took the Great Depression and World War II to provide the energy and focus for the reconstruction that laid the foundation for modern Australia. Will we have to wait for another crash before we find the model that restores stability to our twenty-first century?

SOURCES

"The economy was the primary reason": Malcolm Turnbull, doorstop interview, Canberra, 14 September 2015.

"It was on Abbott's watch": International Monetary Fund, Australia, IMF Country Report No. 15/274, September 2015.

"but this time it didn't": Australia's unemployment rate was 5.6 per cent when the Abbott government came to power in September 2013, 1.7 percentage points below the US unemployment rate of 7.3 per cent. A year later, the lines had crossed, and by September 2015, when Tony Abbott was removed as prime minister, Australia's unemployment rate was 6.1 per cent compared to the US 5.1 per cent. For the Australian data, see: Australian Bureau of Statistics, *Labour Force, Australia,* cat. no. 6202.0, ABS, Canberra, December 2015, table 1. For the US data, see United States Department of Labor, Bureau of Labor Statistics, http://data.bls.gov/timeseries/LNS 14000000.

"The media post-mortems": Peter Hartcher, "Shirtfronted: The story of the Abbott government," *Sydney Morning Herald,* 29 November – 3 December 2015, www.smh.com.au/interactive/2015/Shirtfronted /.

"Mr Speaker, the Abbott government": Joe Hockey's valedictory speech, *Hansard,* 21 October 2015, p.11947.

"We need to restore": Turnbull, 14 September 2015.

"the first Labor leader to win office when the economy was strong": Gough Whitlam, by contrast, took power in December 1972, following a prolonged slowdown in the economy. GDP had contracted in three of the previous four quarters – a recession by any definition. See Australian Bureau of Statistics, *Australian National Accounts:National Income, Expenditure and Product,* cat. no. 5206.0, ABS, Canberra, September 2015, table 2.

"smallest pay rise since the wages system was deregulated": "The through the year rise for the private sector was the smallest rate of wages growth recorded since the start of the series." Australian Bureau of Statistics, *Wage Price Index, Australia,* cat. no. 6345.0, ABS, Canberra, September 2015.

"The unexpected story": Calculations for male and female employment by industry, Australian Bureau of Statistics, *Labour Force, Australia, Detailed, Quarterly,* cat. no. 6291.0.55.003, Canberra, ABS, November 2015, tables 04 and 06.

"Household debt": Reserve Bank of Australia, *Statistical Tables,* www.rba.gov.au/statistics/tables/, table E2, column D.

"Public investment fell": Calculations from ABS, cat. no. 5206.0, table 3.

"Ken Henry explains": Interview with author for the ABC television series *Making Australia Great:Inside Our Longest Boom.* Comments were not broadcast on the show.

"The IMF chided the Abbott government": IMF, *Australia.*

"Joel Deane chronicled the mistakes": Joel Deane, *Catch and Kill: The Politics of Power,* University of Queensland Press, 2015, pp.176–8.

"We are one of just three developed nations": Calculations for employment rates made from OECD, *Short-Term Labour Market Statistics,* http://stats.oecd.org/Index.aspx?DataSetCode=STLABOUR, data extracted on 30 October 2015, 06:33 UTC (GMT) from OECD.Stat.

"In the full employment 1960s": ABS, cat. no. 5206.0, table 24.

"Ken Henry says": Interview with author for *Making Australia Great: Inside Our Longest Boom.* Part of this section of the interview was broadcast in the third episode.

"The dog days for New South Wales": Data for state growth taken from Australian Bureau of Statistics, *Australian National Accounts: State Accounts, 2014–15,* cat. no. 5220.0, ABS, Canberra, 20 November 2015, table 1.

"39 per cent of Sydney's population are overseas-born": Migration statistics taken from Australian Bureau of Statistics, *Australian Social Trends, 2014,* cat. no. 4102.0, ABS, Canberra, 18 March 2014; and from author's calculations based on raw tables from the 2011 census supplied to him by the ABS in August 2012.

"Those that score best": The Economist Intelligence Unit, *A Summary of the Live-ability Ranking and Overview,* August 2014.

"we had something the Chinese wanted": Department of Foreign Affairs and Trade, *Australia's Trade at a Glance,* summary of Australia's trade with China, http://dfat.gov.au/trade/resources/trade-at-a-glance/Pages/default.aspx; US trade with China: United States Census Bureau, *Trade in Goods with China,* www.census.gov/foreign-trade/balance/c5700.html. Note the figures quoted are in Australian and US dollars respectively. Comparison is based on trade in goods only.

"Paul Volcker": Interview with author for *Making Australia Great: Inside Our Longest Boom.* Comments were not broadcast on the show.

"The total tax take": Calculations taken from Australian Government, *Budget 2014–15,* supplementary table 2.

"By 2005–06, it would be $3.8 billion": George Megalogenis, "Tax-as-you-earn workers stung by $3.8bn bracket creep," *Weekend Australian,* 21 February 2004, p.1.

"between $20 billion and $31.5 billion": Ben Phillips and Amar Vohra, "Bracket creep a big factor in Australian living standards," *SAS-Natsem Report,* NATSEM, 18 December 2015.

"If you knew for a fact": Ken Henry, interview with author for *Making Australia Great: Inside Our Longest Boom.* Comments were not broadcast on the show.

"the tax cuts made Australia less fair": Nicolas Herault and Fransisco Azpitarte, "Understanding changes in the distribution and redistribution of income: A unifying decomposition framework," *Review of Income and Wealth,* 12 December 2014.

"John Howard remains unrepentant": Interview with author for *Making Australia Great: Inside Our Longest Boom.* Part of this section of the interview was broadcast in the third episode.

"They saw him being opportunistic": Mark Textor, interview with author for *Making Australia Great: Inside Our Longest Boom.* Comments were not broadcast on the show.

"The most telling article": Dennis Atkins, "No tax unstudied as Malcolm Turnbull's cabinet creates mud map for reform," *Courier-Mail,* 14 November 2015.

"I thought we were very close": Ian Macfarlane, interview with author for *Making Australia Great, Inside Our Longest Boom.* This is an edited version of comments broadcast in the second episode.

"Sydney house prices": Australian Bureau of Statistics, *Residential Property Price Indexes: Eight Capital Cities,* cat. no. 6416.0, ABS, Canberra, September 2015, tables 2 and 3.

"An unintended benefit": Reserve Bank of Australia, *Monetary Policy,* www.rba.gov.au/monetary-policy/– details of Australian official interest rates are summarised under "interest rate decisions." For US and other international official interest rates, see RBA, Statistical Tables, table F13.

"The landlord class": Calculations from Australian Taxation Office, *Taxation Statistics 2012–13,* table 1.

"does that really matter?": Ken Henry, interview with author for *Making Australia Great: Inside Our Longest Boom.* Comments were not broadcast on the show.

"John Quiggin pointed out": John Quiggin, "How New Zealand Fell Further Behind," *Inside Story* (online), 11 November 2015.

"Mark Textor says voters understand": Interview with author for *Making Australia Great: Inside Our Longest Boom.* Comments were not broadcast on the show.

"It was a harbinger": Before 2007, the lowest primary vote for an incoming Labor government was Jim

Scullin's 48.8 per cent in 1929. Kevin Rudd's entry vote was 43.5 per cent and his exit vote in 2013 was 33.4 per cent. The evidence at state level is that the next federal Labor government may return to office with a primary vote below 40 per cent. It has already done this twice in Queensland, in 1988 and 2015, and once each in Western Australia (2001), South Australia (2002) and Victoria (2014). Note that Julia Gillard won minority government in 2010 with a primary vote of 38 per cent, which was 0.8 per cent lower than the primary vote Paul Keating was defeated with in 1996.

"The shifts in global economic power": Calculations from the International Monetary Fund, *World Economic Outlook Database,* October 2015, www.imf.org/www.imf.org/external/pubs/ft/weo/2015/02/weodata/weoselgr.aspx.

"A troubling spike in deaths": Anne Case and Angus Deaton, "Rising morbidity and mortality in midlife among white non-Hispanic Americans in the 21st century," *Proceedings of the National Academy of Sciences of the United States of America,* vol. 112, no. 49, 17 September 2015.

"Professor Bob Gregory has found": Tables supplied by Professor Gregory, which he used for his speech "The Amazing Decade: The Million People Surprise," Social and Economic Outlook Conference, Melbourne, 5 November 2015.

POLITICAL AMNESIA

Correspondence

Bernie Fraser

Many Australians feel let down by some of the institutions that have accompanied them through the twists and turns of their lives. They have discovered that trust in those institutions long taken for granted has too often proved to be misplaced. Governments (at all levels) probably top the list of let-down institutions, but there are others, including corporates (from large financial and mining companies to small convenience stores), trade unions, religious organisations and sporting bodies.

Australians are not alone in feeling aggrieved on this score. There seems to be a widespread betrayal of trust by similar kinds of institutions everywhere, including in many countries we view as sharing our values. The erosion of trust in such institutions is now so deep that even their broader democratic and mixed-economy underpinnings are increasingly looking like damaged goods – less satisfying to countries which have them (Australia and the United States included), and less appealing to countries which might be contemplating them.

For me this is part of the big-picture backdrop to Laura Tingle's excellent essay on political amnesia. Drawing on more than three decades of keen observation and analysis, Laura traces the slide of Australian governments into ordinariness in recent times, its drivers, and the poor policies and lost opportunities that are among its consequences. Having some familiarity with policy-making over this period, I believe Laura's essay provides invaluable insights for anyone trying to comprehend this serious erosion of trust and integrity, and searching for the paths back to good government.

It is the restoration of trust and integrity in the institutions of executive government (cabinet and the ministry) and the parliament that is the major focus of Laura's essay. This seems a good entry point into the broader problem, given both the pervasive influence of these particular institutions and the potential demonstration effect of restoring trust in them on other afflicted institutions.

The "we" in the subtitle "How we forgot how to govern" refers foremost to cabinet ministers but also extends to members of parliament generally, with both cohorts having largely forgotten how differently these institutions functioned in the past. On my reading, Laura's point is not that today's institutions should be recast in their earlier images; given the flaws in those moulds, this would not be a smart thing to do. Rather, the point is that the absence of good memory of how these institutions operated (for good and ill) in the past – the issues they confronted, how they resolved them and the consequences – denies current decision-makers valuable lessons when tackling today's challenges. Insights that might have helped to prevent, for example, a concentration of power in the position of prime minister (with centralised policy and media management and "captain's calls"), dysfunctional cabinet processes and the trivialisation of Question Time.

How these and other shortcomings in current practices can be tied to a loss of institutional memory is well documented in the essay. It all adds up to a very credible thesis. At the same time, other factors have been at work – and are discussed in the essay – which are less directly related to memory loss.

One such factor is feeding "the 24/7 media beast" (Laura's words). Many ministers (and their shadows) seem to relish the endless opportunities to comment on their portfolios (and sometimes on their colleagues' portfolios as well) and to have a dig at their opponents. Mostly they recycle old assertions and slogans about, for example, the dire consequences of budget deficits and carbon prices; rarely do they emit useful new information. Of likely more concern to viewers of these sessions is confirmation of their suspicions that the community would be better served if the ministerial time and effort now devoted to these activities were to be redirected to getting on top of real issues, and to forging sustainable policies, in the cabinet room.

A second and obvious factor, which is partly related to questions of political memory and process, is the quality and depth of the ministry and its capacity to function as an effective team. Comparisons here, like comparing thoroughbreds of different eras, are matters of judgment. In my book, based on observations extending over the past fifty years, the Hawke cabinet of the 1980s would have a big lead on all the others to have gone around before and since that time.

Prime Minister Turnbull seems to have recognised that recent governments have let down lots of Australians, both in some of the policies adopted and the processes surrounding the determination and communication of those policies. The prime minister has foreshadowed changes to help restore trusted and open government to Australians, including the replacement of on-the-run decision-making and captain's calls with more traditional cabinet processes.

These good intentions warrant strong community support, and will probably require that if they are to be realised.

Another change promised by the prime minister is better government engagement with the bureaucracy in policy-making. This is a critical relationship crying out for urgent repair. Personal experience – as well as common sense – tells me that effective working relationships between diligent ministers and diligent departments make for good outcomes. In the second half of the 1980s, for example, Treasury had a close

– if not always frictionless – working relationship with Treasurer Keating, which, I believe, contributed to some significant reforms during that period. (For their own reasons, a couple of journalists of the day choose to denigrate this cooperation, calling it "politicisation" (and worse) of the Treasury; these comments drew a firm rebuttal from Malcolm Fraser – never a fan of the Treasury – who applauded the close relationship and lamented its absence during his time as prime minister.)

Many relationships, of course, have not worked out. For various reasons, different ministers and governments have lacked confidence in the capacity of their bureaucrats to provide appropriate advice, at least of the kinds some would prefer to receive. As recorded in Laura's essay, the erosion of trust in these relationships has built up over the years. Elected in 1972, the Whitlam government was unsure of the loyalty it might receive from a bureaucracy that had served only Coalition governments for twenty-five years: it prepared itself by appointing a number of "outsiders" to positions in departments and in the offices of incoming ministers. These practices were continued, fairly incrementally, in subsequent administrations before taking off to new levels in the Howard and Abbott governments, when significant numbers of senior bureaucrats were replaced and staffs of ministerial offices inflated in a quest for more accommodating advice.

These and other changes – including widespread outsourcing of government activities – appear to have so diminished the public service that it no longer has the capacity, the opportunity and perhaps even the spirit to play its critical role in upholding the standard of public policy-making. As Laura has noted: "we as a community have ceased to recognise what a valuable repository of memory, and what a valuable institution, the public service is."

This situation should be of real concern to every Australian. Today's world is much more fluid than ever before, with unprecedented cross-border flows not only of goods and services, and capital and labour, but also of technologies and ideas, terrorists and refugees, drugs and viruses, warming temperatures and changing climatic patterns. These global and geopolitical developments bring new dimensions and complexities to Australian policy-making in many fields. In their own interests, and certainly in the interests of the communities they represent (who bear the brunt of poor decisions), our leaders need to receive the best possible advice. They will – and should – call on different sources, but the public service should be very prominent in the mix: it should, I suggest, be the government's "go-to" adviser in most instances.

Given its natural perspective and priority (serving the national public interest), its multi-disciplinary cover, and its substantial (if threatened) memory, the public service (with other public sector advisory bodies) has the potential to provide expert and balanced advice of a breadth and depth others would be hard-pressed to match. All that is needed to realise that potential is for it to be adequately resourced; to be managed as a premier advisory institution (not some kind of "business"); and to be viewed by ministers and governments as a respected and indispensable partner in policy-making.

To help rebuild trust in Australia's governmental institutions, Prime Minister Turnbull has spoken of the need for a public service which works better and engages better with ministers. Changes in these areas are overdue and, again, Turnbull's good intentions should be supported and pursued vigorously. To this end, the prime minister himself could do worse than commission a comprehensive and independent review to propose appropriate structures and responsibilities for Australia's public service in today's new world. It would likely find many clues in the old ground turned over so diligently by Laura Tingle in her essay.

Bernie Fraser

POLITICAL AMNESIA

Correspondence

Amanda Walsh

Laura Tingle's autopsy of policy-making in the Australian Public Service is accurate and revealing. I write as one of the Class of '96, that generation of public servants reared entirely in the Howard era, when policy-making disappeared from APS departments. Tingle notes that the Department of Foreign Affairs and Trade was spared the worst of the policy vacuuming – but it didn't seem that way to me, as a fresh-faced newcomer. While DFAT is renowned as one of a handful of "elite" agencies in the APS, it was clear throughout the Howard years that policy-making was simply not in its remit.

I vividly recall sitting in a large function room in Canberra in 1995, preparing to sit one of the many DFAT entrance exams. With a twinkle in his eye, the official administering the exam provided some advice on the recruitment process: "Don't tell us you want to join up for the policy work – we know it's all about the overseas postings!" This was met with hearty laughter from the assembled university students, but it triggered a small alarm in my brain. "But I *am* in it for the policy work," I thought, and I'm sure I wasn't the only one.

My subsequent career in DFAT presented me with many unique opportunities and lots of fun – but no policy work, not really. My overseas posting at least gave me the opportunity to write reporting cables – but I was not in an "important" part of the world, so my reports disappeared into the encryption system and landed in front of an invisible, mute audience. In three years, only one reader ever piped up to begin a dialogue about my policy analysis. (That person is now a senior public servant in the Department of the Prime Minister & Cabinet – so perhaps there is hope!)

With the notable exception of the highly technical work of our negotiators in the World Trade Organization's Doha Round, DFAT simply didn't "do" policy in the late 1990s and the early years of the new millennium. The centralisation of policy work in ministerial offices – combined with foreign minister Alexander Downer's open loathing of the APS – created an environment in which DFAT jumped when asked, but otherwise stood still. There was no culture of inquiry, let alone policy debate. Junior staff (many with qualifications in international relations and experience working overseas) prepared meeting agendas and ferried visiting dignitaries to expensive restaurants and outback tourist haunts. Hey, it's a living.

It dawned on me gradually that policy-making wasn't going to be part of my career. This was more than a little deflating. So I started a postgraduate research degree in my spare time. I worked at DFAT by day and analysed policy by night. The irony was not lost on me. I can reel off a list of former colleagues – all stunningly bright and personable – who left DFAT around the time I did. Without exception, they beat a path to policy-based work: in academia, think-tanks or politics.

I should emphasise that the problem of failing policy nous in the APS (as ably described by Tingle) is not confined to DFAT. I did try my hand at a designated "policy" job in the public service a few years later. This was in a portfolio closely related to my PhD studies, and I was hopeful of making a proper contribution there. The work quickly revealed itself to be mostly administrative – until the day a very senior executive phoned me in a flap to say that the newly minted minister wanted "some ideas for new policies." I was given *two days* to throw together a list of proposals. There was no input from seasoned policy experts in the department – because they didn't exist. Two days later, the senior executive professed herself delighted with my bare-boned list, which was duly despatched to the minister's office. We didn't hear back. Well, I don't think we did – I quietly resigned a few weeks later. The APS is just no place for policy-making anymore.

Amanda Walsh

Correspondence

Tarah Barzanji

At heart, the problem is one of accountability. Accountability for policy development no longer lies with the public service. Instead, it is often within the purview of the ministerial staffer or the party's election policy committee. Without doubt, we want our governments and staffers to provide a touchstone or framework for policy development, and to outline the values that policies should advance. And it is entirely appropriate for a new government to bring urgency for change and an appetite for reform. But detailed policy design by ministerial staffers is probably not healthy.

While I was working in Prime Minister Rudd's office, I thought it was to the credit of our policy advisers that briefs did not obsessively focus on political sensitivities. Instead, sensitivities comprised a short section and were often de-emphasised amid complex policy discussion. Now I wonder if our large and very capable staff should have been less instrumental in policy design.

Ideally, we want our public service to be an engine room for ideas, which are then modified according to the values of the current government. But until the public service gets a clear message that it should be "open for policy business," it will struggle to attract and retain the talent required to develop both good ideas and institutional memory.

Centralised decision-making concentrates power in an ever-smaller group, within a very large public service. By many accounts, Prime Minister Turnbull appears to be returning government to a more decentralised status quo. A friend in his office confirms that he has strong intentions to run a cabinet government. When considering a brief from his office, Turnbull quips, "I'll need to ask the opinion of my health adviser," referring to the Minister for Health.

Less centralised decision-making should help with another of Tingle's laments: that all ministers and parliamentary secretaries are viewed (by the government and the media) as mouthpieces on any topic, rather than experts in their policy area. Indeed, the talking points that we distributed each morning from Prime Minister Rudd's office were called "Round-the-worlds," in recognition that any member of government could get a question on any topic.

Finally, we should be alert for "institutional memory" masking an underlying resistance to change. Occasionally in my time at the Department of Prime Minister and Cabinet, I noticed that we would brief against a policy because we had a vague institutional memory of a similar policy being debated and rejected in the past. As a recent graduate, I took this as received wisdom. But looking back, it may just have been institutional inertia.

So while memory is useful, we should be careful that it is not used merely to maintain the status quo. Indeed, in some areas it may be helpful to start afresh. Some of the most interesting social policy ideas around the world at the moment are emerging from radical breaks with traditional ways of thinking and operating. Rather than a plaything of the rich or the supergeeks, technology is being reconceived as a way to drive inclusion, prevention and opportunity.

Institutional memory may help to drive policy strength in the public service, but it might not serve governments equally well in embracing the new.

Tarah Barzanji

POLITICAL AMNESIA

Correspondence

Allan Behm

Like the Quarterly Essay, papal encyclicals deal with matters of contemporary moment. In 1958, Pius XII issued *Meminisse iuvat* ("It Helps to Remember"), addressing the plight of the Church in Eastern Europe. No doubt he was channelling Ovid, just as Laura Tingle has in the dedication appended to her excellent and very sobering encyclical. But while the Pope employed the consoling language of prayer and the imagery of an ancient iconography, Tingle has delivered a much more forensic and mordant account of the dysfunctional nature of modern Australian government.

For those of us who cannot remember whether we have amnesia or not, it is confronting to have the trite and ephemeral character of our national politics so ruthlessly flensed and filleted. It is as though we are doomed to live in a Kafkaesque present that comes from nowhere and goes to the same place. And for someone like me, who spent three decades grappling with the major themes of foreign, defence and national security policy, not to mention a subsequent four years wrestling with climate change policy as a chief of staff in the Rudd and Gillard governments, it forces the unanswerable question, "Why did I waste my life like that?"

Yet political amnesia is not new. We simply do not care to remember it, thereby permitting its constant repetition. Just three years before the Anschluss that helped to set Europe on its path to hell, in a famous speech attacking German rearmament, Churchill commented on the futile Stresa agreement between Britain, France and Italy.

> When the situation was manageable it was neglected, and now that it is thoroughly out of hand we apply too late the remedies which then might have effected a cure. There is nothing new in the story. It is as old as the sibylline books. It falls into that long, dismal catalogue of the fruitlessness of experience and the confirmed unteachability of mankind. Want of foresight, unwillingness to act when action would be simple and effective, lack of clear thinking, confusion of counsel until the emergency comes, until self-preservation strikes its jarring gong – these are the features which constitute the endless repetition of history.

He could have been talking about Australia's experience.

If one cannot trace the lineage of a policy, placing it in the broader narrative of history, then it will lack relevance and durability. The troubled story of

Australia's climate change policy offers a poignant example of this. It was not so much the inability of the Gillard government adequately to explain its policy as it was Abbott's refusal to countenance Howard's slow but steady journey to the Damascus of a price on carbon that destroyed a market-based approach to tackling global warming. The inane repetition of "Axe the tax" failed to distinguish between a tax and a price. More importantly, the trashing of the Clean Energy Future package both deprived Australia of an economically efficient means of reducing the atmospheric carbon burden and destroyed our reputation as a progressive and constructive member of a community of like-minded nations intent upon creating a global solution to "the greatest moral challenge of our generation" – and all this for a short-term political victory that was inevitable. It is a delicious irony that the victor is now himself vanquished, joining his soulmate, Canada's recently repudiated prime minister, Stephen Harper, in the pit that is amnesia's doppelganger – oblivion.

But the etiology of Australia's governmental paralysis does not depend on amnesia alone. Tingle weaves at least three other symptoms of dysfunction into her lament for a broken system.

First, the hollowing out of the public service, with the consequent loss of institutional memory, has contributed enormously to our political amnesia.

Second, the rise of the political class has effectively promoted personal political preferment over the national interest, or even the interests of the party. While Labor boasts a greater collection of dunderheads (especially in the Senate) who have arm-wrestled their way through the union movement, the Liberal and National parties are not immune from the careerists and crazy-braves unable to distinguish between pragmatism and principle. For the political class, the tide of history is no help in surfing the wave of the moment.

And third, the arrival of the political staffer – reflecting the need of many politicians to surround themselves with adolescent claqueurs rather than experienced counsellors – reinforces the triumph of evanescence over substance. The half-life of the average political staffer is about two years, with changes in ministerial appointment and, more particularly, changes in government precipitating major clean-outs. As Tingle reflects throughout her essay, churn is the enemy of continuity. It, too, causes political amnesia.

This amnesia, however, is reinforced by a number of equally pernicious developments that could be added to Tingle's list.

Chief among these, at least until Turnbull's resurrection as prime minister, has been the absence of any articulated vision for Australia, or even for the government of the day. The electorate simply has no idea what the government aspires to, what it stands for or what its values might be. The recurrent slogans of "queue jumpers," "they're coming to get us," "the economy's a wreck," "we pay too much tax" and "small government" betray a craven inability to imagine a future that improves upon the past. This is not just amnesia – it is cynicism.

Second, leadership is the vehicle that delivers vision. That, too, is in deficit. The sight of prime ministers lurching from one self-generated crisis to another serves both to undermine the confidence of the electorate and to reinforce the popular view that we are governed by hollow men and women. One of Howard's strengths was to manage the news cycle, rather than being managed by it. Rudd, Gillard and Abbott all failed to assert the authority of their office, preferring to start at shadows or manufacture "announcements" that were little more than a recycling program to an electorate that couldn't be bothered remembering what might have been said yesterday.

A third factor that contributes to Australia's political malaise is a rejection of reform, less a result of reform fatigue (the past decade has not seen enough reform to tire anyone) than of reform phobia. And where reform has been attempted, such as the Clean Energy Future package managed through the parliament by Greg Combet (more an economic reform than an environmental one, it should be noted), it has been unceremoniously dumped by fear-mongering ideologues.

A final and even more cynical contribution to the mess that is contemporary Australian government is the disdain for effective accountability. A procession of ministers, for instance, has hidden behind the fiction of "operational security" in refusing to comment on so-called "on-water matters" when questioned about the plight of refugees and detainees.

The Abbott government's draconian Border Force Act made it a criminal offence for anyone working for or contracted to the Department of Immigration and Border Protection to reveal anything that happens at the offshore detention centres. This effectively removes an element of public administration costing over $1 billion per annum from parliamentary and media scrutiny, morphing it into a quasi-security operation. The black uniforms and martial tone sit oddly with Turnbull's new emphasis on reconciliation, inclusiveness and engagement.

And the security organisations, never especially accountable, have themselves become even less accountable for the actions of their employees, who are now indemnified against prosecution if they commit a crime in the course of a "special security operation."

The 2001 Children Overboard affair and the subsequent parliamentary inquiries showed that ministerial staffers are not accountable. While public servants are subject to a biannual pummelling at the hands of inquisitorial senators, ministerial advisors are not answerable for their actions or for the policy advice they provide to their ministers. This is symptomatic of the pathology modern governments have towards any form of accountability, whether it is media scrutiny or parliamentary review. Yet accountability is central to a vibrant and robust democracy. It is also a powerful stimulant to memory.

In 1979, John Paul II issued his first encyclical, *Redemptor hominis* ("Mankind's Redeemer"), offering the promise of redemption as the solution to the doubt, crisis and collapse affecting the contemporary church. We should all look forward to Tingle's third encyclical in the hope that it will inspire confidence and optimism that our governmental system is on the mend. To that end, Cicero's *De Officiis* ("Concerning Responsibilities," often mistranslated as "On Duties") may be a more instructive text than the *Annales* of Tacitus.

Allan Behm

POLITICAL AMNESIA

Correspondence

Jennifer Rayner

If the one-eyed man is king among the blind, what does that make the keeper of memories in a country of alleged amnesiacs? Seriously and permanently exasperated, if Laura Tingle's *Political Amnesia* is anything to go by.

Tingle began covering national politics before many of we "meretricious players" now populating Parliament House were born. The number of people who know more than she does about the contemporary political and policy history of Australia could fit around the dining table at the Lodge.

Having borne witness to Australian politics at some of its greatest modern moments of achievement and ambition, it is not surprising that Tingle would look reproachfully upon the past six years. Between their echoing codas of "wild treachery and weirdness," and the claustrophobic tug of war that has seen barely a metre of progress gained on key policy issues, these must often have been dispiriting times to cover from up close.

But in searching for ways to put all that behind us, Tingle may be looking in the wrong place. By placing such emphasis on political memory, her essay implicitly asserts that the past is an accurate guide to the present; that "what worked then" should influence us – public servants, politicians and advisers – when making decisions about "what to do now." She writes: "Without memory, there is no context or continuity for the making of new decisions ... The perils of this are manifest. Decisions are taken that are not informed by knowledge of what has worked, or not worked, in the past."

At the same time, Tingle acknowledges that the environment in which politicians seek to govern is very different now than it was twenty or thirty years ago. She focuses on changes in the media landscape and their effect on the daily practice of politics, but a series of broader shifts beyond the walls of parliament and the press gallery also need to be acknowledged. Taken together, they make today's political environment so different from the Howard years – and certainly from any prior era – that it is questionable whether we can gain all that much from mining the successes and stuff-ups of those earlier times. The really significant changes include:

The decline of government expertise and authority

Where once governments could speak to the people with an authoritative voice (and public service agencies to their ministers with the same), there are now many and competing sources of information, knowledge and opinion. Put simply, citizens in democracies don't believe or trust their governments just because they are The Government anymore. The mistrust that started with Watergate and the Dismissal, and grew through events like the Iraq War and the global financial crisis, has seen to that; not to mention local outrages like Children Overboard and the steady drip of entitlement scandals, broken promises and internecine brawls that have worn holes in the credibility of office.

The result is that every idea, every argument, every policy must be developed and prosecuted in an environment that can sometimes resemble a free-fire zone. Competing ideas and information from lobby groups, academics and every wingnut with an internet connection are constantly whizzing by, while media outlets – whom Tingle rightly identifies as increasingly relentless – are hunting for any crack in the plaster before it has even set.

The GST debate was a glaring example of this. By my count, no fewer than seven organisations or individuals – the Greens; David Gillespie MP; Grattan

Institute; Deloitte Access Economics; Pricewaterhouse-Coopers; Parliamentary Budget Office; CPA Australia – recently published detailed and diverse modelling on ways to change the GST and its impact on household budgets. There's no doubt this adds contestability to the debate, but it has also seen the Liberal government lose control of the tax reform conversation in a way that will make laying out a coherent policy direction mighty difficult (should it ever find the *cojones* to do so).

When the voice of government no longer carries a decisive weight in political debate, setting a policy course and steering true takes far more effort and skill than was required of past administrations.

The personalisation and customisation of service delivery

After decades of being told we are not citizens but "clients," people have internalised this message. As a result, consumers of government services now expect to be king at the Medicare office just as much as they are at Myer. Gone are the days when governments could dictate to Australians how and when their offerings should be accessed, or cleanly delimit their areas of responsibility. As the Department of Finance noted: "citizens are not concerned about which agencies or levels of government deliver the services they require; they increasingly expect coordinated responses that they can access in any way they choose."

The behind-the-scenes coordination and information-sharing needed to make this happen is diabolically complicated. The introduction of the National Disability Insurance Scheme is Australia's first serious attempt to deliver truly tailored services on a national scale. Instead of block-funding services that people with disability must take or leave, the scheme offers custom-designed care packages that let consumers themselves decide what sort of supports they need. Successfully delivering this scheme to the half a million Australians who may ultimately be eligible for it will require an unprecedented level of coordination between state and federal governments, as well as among government agencies at both levels. It is a clear departure from the one-size-fits-most approach.

Whether or not the NDIS succeeds according to its original vision, this is what service delivery will be expected to look like in the future. No past Australian administration – not Howard's, not Keating's or Hawke's before him – ever faced a populace with such high or varied expectations of how government would serve it.

The triple bottom line

Tingle writes somewhat witheringly of Kevin Rudd's commitment to achieving the "double dividend" of economic and environmental good when designing Australia's response to the global financial crisis. But in fact, almost all policies are now expected to take some account of the "triple bottom line" of economic, environmental and social impacts. In particular, growing awareness over the past two decades of environmental harms such as climate change and, more recently, social challenges such as inequality, mean that governments must grapple with solving specific problems while ensuring their solutions also address – or at least do not exacerbate – these more general ones.

Energy policy needs not only to deal with practicalities like pricing or supply, but also to lower Australia's carbon emissions. Infrastructure investment must boost productivity while remedying service gaps that have fostered inequalities across our cities. Health policy should make us fitter and healthier, and do so in ways that deliver long-term efficiencies to the budget.

It was far simpler to design and deliver policies back when the only things that mattered were their primary impacts: how many people helped, how much money spent, what contribution to the nation's capital stock?

In short then, the present political environment bears about as much resemblance to that of the early Howard years as Kim Kardashian does to Kim Beazley. Today's governments have weaker authority, but are expected to do more for us and fix more complex problems. All this, while having less direct control over key economic levers and being increasingly hemmed in by events and agreements set in train far from our shores.

Australia's recent administrations are of course not alone in facing these challenges. In light of this, it seems that asking, "What worked here, before?" will not necessarily unearth the useful insights Tingle has advocated for in her essay. A better question for those seeking to make sound policy may be, "What is working now, elsewhere?"

Rather than studying the rear-view mirror, we should be looking overseas, to other jurisdictions around Australia, to any place where they have faced the same problems we wish to solve and successfully surmounted them *in today's political environment.* For example, Canada has a long-term unemployment rate less than half of Australia's – what can we learn from it about policies that get people back to work and keep them there? Germany's share of world service exports is five times greater than Australia's – what might we glean from its success and apply to our own economy? Victorian school kids routinely perform better on standardised tests like NAPLAN than their confreres elsewhere – what should we borrow from that state's approach to lift standards across the nation?

To gather promising policies, magpie-like, we do not necessarily need public servants with long institutional memories. However, we certainly do need a smart, analytically rigorous APS staffed by the sharpest talent this country can produce.

Tingle is spot-on in arguing that continual cuts and disrespect are no way to build a public service of this calibre. But if we can recruit the best people and put them to work in well-resourced agencies held in high esteem by politicians and the public alike, their mission once there should not be to delve inwards and into the past. It must be to look outwards to policy successes elsewhere and in the present.

Jennifer Rayner

POLITICAL AMNESIA

Correspondence

Anne Tiernan

Hugh Heclo describes government agencies as "bundles of memory and practices that are inherited from a particular past and carried forward." Laura Tingle's Quarterly Essay confirms this: an institution's memory lies partly in its traditions – in its processes of socialisation and the stories that are told and retold from one generation to the next. Seldom is such knowledge written down. Much of it is tacit, known informally and passed on verbally. It is learnt through apprenticeship and refined through practice and experience.

Many observers (including the chiefs of staff and senior officials I have interviewed) believe that institutional memory is now under threat. In Westminster systems, the bureaucracy's rationale is to provide continuity of administration and institutional memory for governments, whatever their political hue. Instead we have what British political scientist Christopher Pollitt describes as "organisational forgetting." Of course, as we have seen, there is nothing neutral about institutional memory; politics is inherent to judgments about what to remember and what to forget – hence the ferocity of the history wars that were once waged between the political parties, but now rage within them – including, as we have seen since 2010, and as Malcolm Turnbull is learning to his chagrin, within incumbent governments.

Laura has taken what was until now an academic and insider debate and made it accessible to an informed readership. She builds a compelling and mostly persuasive case. Our political institutions and policy processes have become debased to the point where a large proportion of Australia's citizens, its business and community leaders now seriously doubts their capacity to address current and future challenges. I strongly concur with her diagnosis that this is the unintended consequence of more than forty years of almost continuous "reform." She is so right when she observes that, "we have not at any point stopped to look back and frankly assess what has been good and what has been bad, and whether we need to change not just policy but the way we think about entire issues, and how we think about the role of the public sector."

I am less convinced that problems delivering the Rudd government's stimulus programs in response to the global financial crisis were attributable to a lack of memory within the Commonwealth public service about how to implement large capital programs. I contend that this exposed a quite different kind of forgetting – one that is much more pervasive and troubling. It seems to me Australia's political class and the press gallery no longer remembers what constitutes an appropriate role for the federal government. Successive reviews and inquiries have shown that much of the necessary expertise was available at the state level. As with so many recent Commonwealth forays into areas of state responsibility, this expertise was neither sought nor heard. The issue, then, was less one of institutional memory than of habit and culture among Commonwealth ministers and their departments in their dealings with their sub-national counterparts; and a lack of respect for the "rules of the game" about who can and should do what within Australia's federal system.

Laura's provocative questions are "Can we fix it?" and "Where does it lead us if we don't?" I have argued elsewhere that ministers are the missing link in public sector reform. We have a structural problem that, in many ways, ministers have brought on themselves. The hybrid model that emphasised responsiveness, that has led to centralisation, small group decision-making and a tendency to focus on the short term, has begun to fray and show its limits. Political leaders are failing to learn the lessons of experience – theirs and others – and it is costing them.

The question is how to build a plank of continuity into the arrangements of government. The United States has been grappling with this dilemma for sixty years. It is a fruitful source of ideas for mechanisms to enhance institutional memory. In the American parlance, the goal of every new administration is to "hit the ground running." Yet few incoming presidents have been able to make the most of the opportunities that present briefly at their transition to government. What Terry Sullivan has called the "triple curses of arrogance, adrenaline and naiveté" can afflict electoral winners, making it difficult fbor them to absorb the lessons of past experience. Yet learning is crucial, to facilitate a smooth and successful transition and to avoid repeating mistakes that can have long-term consequences for a new administration.

In the United States, scholars and practitioners have made two major efforts to address the problem of institutional memory in the White House. The first are studies of the president's chief of staff, where former occupants of the position, from both sides of politics, come together to share insights and lessons from their time in office. The published outcomes of such projects provide "primers" for current and prospective White House staff. The second is an ongoing research collaboration, the White House Transition Project, which provides non-partisan advice and information intended to support an incoming administration to make a smooth transition to government. Its findings are available on a dedicated website: whitehousetransitio nproject.org.

Such detailed empirical work into the roles and functions of the Australian prime minister's office and the offices of senior ministers and other key office holders is perhaps less necessary here than in the American context, where many thousands of positions are filled by political appointees at the start of a new administration. Even if diminished, a professional and impartial career public service remains a potential source of institutional memory – available to all leaders, should they choose to engage it. But, as Laura has shown, this will require significant renovation, including the fashioning of a new narrative tradition that would enable the public service to transcend the serious damage wrought by the disruptive changes of recent years and the behaviour of political and some bureaucratic leaders.

A generation of public servants no longer knows or understands the "rules of the game" because these rules have been violated or dismantled. In the words of the legendary mandarin Sir Arthur Tange, the "symmetry" of the Westminster model has been fractured and not replaced. We know from research that there is no agreement on either the stewardship role of the public service or what now constitutes a "proper" relationship between ministers and public servants. This is a live debate in the UK, where civil servants have identified the relationship with ministers as the "unresolved constitutional question."

Focused effort is needed to recover the craft of public administration. We need, too, to broker a new bargain between ministers, their staff and public servants, where the default is trust, mutual respect and a commitment to work together in the public interest.

In Australia, Rod Rhodes and I have suggested that the search to preserve institutional memory could begin with a review of the arrangements for ministerial staffers. This hybrid system has evolved through accretion rather than design. We might consider other models which ensure that prime ministers get the mix of responsive and neutral competence that they need to discharge their complex obligations. We could ask, for example, whether a politically appointed Senior Executive Service, in preference to ministerial staffers, could help to improve links between ministers and the public service. Other systems cope with politicised public service appointments by requiring candidates to be subject to confirmation processes, for example.

Other options might include considering whether Australian prime ministers might be better served by longer, more formal transition periods. In the US, the period between the election and Inauguration Day is seventy-five days. It's unlikely so long a period would be required (or tolerated by our hyper-partisans), but something a bit longer than the current "morning after the night before" might be worth contemplating – not least because, as we know from Kevin Rudd's experience, and perhaps too from Tony Abbott's, exhausted people taking the reins after a frenetic and bitter election campaign may not make the best decisions. It may be worth considering, too, formal support for transition planning, as has been the case in the United States since 1963.

There remains a fundamental dilemma about how to reconcile responsiveness and agility with experience and institutional memory. Laura has made the case for why we need a wide-ranging debate about how we can learn to remember. So urgent has the loss of institutional memory become that Rod Rhodes and I have argued that the next wave of public-sector reforms should focus on ways of preserving it.

Anne Tiernan

POLITICAL AMNESIA

Correspondence

Graham Evans

Australia faces a set of very difficult challenges, and it has less control over the effectiveness of its responses than has historically been the case. Laura Tingle is right to point out that the explanations frequently given for the decline in policymaking in Australia – the 24-hour news cycle, poll-driven policy options, the rise of the political professional, and the decline of "real life" experience among politicians – are not by themselves sufficient. Her essay also focuses on loss of memory in politics and policy-making, and the collapse of institutions that should be responsible for these, including a risk-averse public service. These are, for her, key factors in explaining the widespread view of those interested in politics and policy that Australia is suffering from "political amnesia," and has forgotten how to govern.

Bob Hawke's government is viewed as one of the most talented and effective in recent decades. It had a well-qualified and diverse group of ministers, especially at the outset. It also had a clear view of the structure and processes of government, much of which had been developed by Gareth Evans. I had the opportunity, when co-opted from the public service to be Hawke's first chief of staff (or principal private secretary), to see this at first-hand. Hawke made it clear from the start that he wanted to govern on the basis of consistent principles:

- Policy decisions were to be made in an orderly way by cabinet, based on the best available advice and cognisant of the views of interested parties, and subsequently ministers were to be responsible for implementing these decisions.
- The prime minister's office was expected to ensure that the policy and political advice to the prime minister was consistent with the government's objectives and was thorough and timely, but at the end of the day the prime minister was the decision-maker.
- The prime minister's office, and indeed the whole of government, needed to work with the public service to make full use of its resources. The public service needed to be involved in developing policy options, not least because it generally had to implement them.

I had the opportunity to speak recently with Hawke. He said, not surprisingly, that none of his views on these elementary but enduring principles had changed, and they remained equally applicable in 2015, despite the many technological and structural changes affecting government that had occurred in subsequent decades.

Tingle raises two matters that are worthy of more detailed comment: the prime minister's office, and the role of the public service. This is not to claim for either that all worked well in "the good old days." Demonstrably this was not the case. Nor is it to say these models are readily applicable to a very different world. But there can be important lessons from the past.

Hawke's four chiefs of staff were all seconded from the public service. But his staff always included senior political advisers who, inter alia, provided views on policy options and certainly had no qualms about putting their views strongly. I was accountable for ensuring this interaction happened. Hawke did not like surprises as a result of inadequate consultation.

The reconciliation of policy and politics was helped by Hawke being clear on the difference between leading and managing, meaning he was prepared to take on issues that were unpopular. "We are here to make a difference," he would say. Most of his ministers were the same. One of them stressed to me after he was appointed Minister for Transport and Communications that he wanted the department always to provide first-best policy options, and he would decide on the politics.

A difficulty I see with the current arrangements for prime ministerial, and indeed ministerial, staff is the larger numbers involved. Hawke's office was able to function with a third of the staff of recent prime ministers. Too many staff inevitably means competition for access to the prime minister, and there is less incentive to use the public service effectively.

Tingle describes at length the way in which significant parts of the public service have suffered a decline in skills and institutional memory. Many blame the growth in the size and influence of ministerial offices for this decline. This is no doubt a contributing factor because little encouragement is given them to work together effectively. But ultimately this is an issue on which leadership has to come from the top. Unless the prime minister of the day is clear about how he or she expects ministerial offices and the public service to work together, it will not happen.

Hawke made this point by making regular visits to the Department of Prime Minister and Cabinet, as did other Hawke government ministers. As Hawke's chief of staff I spoke to Mike Codd and Geoff Yeend as secretaries of the Department of Prime Minister and Cabinet a couple of times each day.

Institutional memory is an interesting concept. How individuals recall the past influences how they act in the present. Hawke's belief that the Whitlam government had not used the public service well affected how he saw that relationship. It is also often the case that public servants in the same institutions for lengthy periods are most resistant to policy change.

Companies often have a different view of institutional memory to the public sector – they don't want their executives to take institutional memory with them if they leave for a competitor. This is generally reflected in employment contracts, and extended "gardening leave" for departing executives.

The challenge for the public service, as Tingle's essay highlights, is how best to learn from the past. But there are other fundamental considerations at work. Central to having governments use the public service effectively, and to attracting good people, is to involve public servants from the outset in the development of policy and its implementation. At present public servants are often brought into the process late or not at all, and yet are expected to implement the policy.

Public servants are also increasingly risk-averse, because they are blamed for mistakes, not always of their own making, that get into the public fora. Of course they should be held accountable for avoidable failures. But if public servants are expected to be more innovative and less risk-averse, there needs to be clarity from the start as to both responsibility and accountability. The shift to greater use of contracts for the public service has only exacerbated the inclination to be risk-averse. A recent Victorian auditor-general's report into the East-West Link included the following observation: "Some public servants involved in this audit indicated that providing frank and fearless advice when they believe a government does not want to receive it will negatively impact their influence or career opportunities."

Policy change is always difficult. The losers know who they will be, but the winners are frequently not aware until after the changes have been made. Vested interests, whether corporate or union, are aggressive and sophisticated in protecting their positions. If governments are to achieve significant reform, the community needs to be engaged and informed of the benefits. While ministers need to play the main role, some part of this responsibility will fall to the public servants, and so progress will involve some risk-taking. The public servants involved in the major changes to communication and transport in the late 1980s and early 1990s can vouch for this, but the productivity gains continue to flow to the economy. In my view the capacity to reform transport and communications existed in the public service in the late 1980s. When it was galvanised by a political commitment to microeconomic reform, and the public service was engaged and worked closely with ministers, reform happened.

Political Amnesia should provoke serious consideration of more effective ways of governing modern Australia, and if it does this it will have been an important contribution to tackling the tough challenges we face.

Graham Evans

POLITICAL AMNESIA

Correspondence

John Quiggin

Laura Tingle is right to suggest that memory is a problem in Australian politics. But, for most of the Australian political class, the problem is not amnesia. Rather, like the Bourbons, they have learned nothing and forgotten nothing.

The key word here is "reform." As Tingle observes, "reform" remains a fetish word, at least for the political class. Its continuing magical power can be seen in the recent National Reform Summit, jointly sponsored by our rival national dailies, the *Australian* and the *Australian Financial Review,* along with the inevitable participation of consulting firm KPMG (which helpfully notes its affiliation with KPMG International, "a Swiss entity").

The content of "reform" is generally taken to be self-explanatory. Obviously, for example, anyone who suggested a tax reform that would require higher income earners to pay more income tax, or a productivity reform that involved more leisure, would not have been welcome.

As Tingle observes, "reform" has become "a hollowed-out word which you attach to anything voters won't like in the hope that it will make you appear a strong and decisive government." The problem lies in her implicit contrast with an earlier era in which there was consensus around a reform agenda based on an "obligation to explain and advocate."

The memory of this golden era is what gives the word "reform" its continuing magical power, at least among the political class. But it is largely mythical. Reform has been a top-down process, imposed without any serious attempt at persuasion, from the very beginning. The floating of the dollar, generally seen as the starting point of the microeconomic reform era, was announced following late-night meetings between Treasurer Keating and senior Treasury officials, the content of which is still disputed.

By the early 1990s, the term "economic rationalism" had entered the public lexicon, thanks to Michael Pusey's book *Economic Rationalism in Canberra.* The era of explanation and advocacy was well and truly over, replaced by a sharp divide between the political class and the public. As Tingle observes (with implicit reference to the political class), to argue against economic rationalism was to invite "ridicule or contempt." By contrast, among the public at large "economic rationalist" became, and remains, a term of abuse.

The results were seen in the National Competition Policy (NCP), a deliberate and successful attempt to institutionalise economic reform by means of an endrun around the political process. A carefully selected committee, appointed to analyse an obscure area of commercial law, produced recommendations which turned into an intergovernmental agreement, backed with huge and financial incentives and penalties. By the time NCP came to the attention of the ordinary voter (through, for example, the contracting out of local government services), it was a fait accompli, impossible to challenge through any democratic process.

The upsurge of support for Pauline Hanson was not only due to John Howard's dog-whistle attacks on "political correctness." It owed at least as much to the (correct) perception that ordinary people no longer had any say in the crucial issues of economic policy. Tingle recognises this, but, like the rest of the political class, treats it as an unalterable fact about the world rather than the result of specific (and misguided) policy choices.

John Quiggin

POLITICAL AMNESIA

Correspondence

Scott Ludlam

Laura Tingle's thoughtful and at times sombre portrait of the politics of amnesia touched a nerve for me, principally because, as if to prove her point, there was so much in the essay I wasn't aware of. Modern Australian political history tends to canvas the sharp break-points and scandals, leaving slower-moving institutional dynamics as vague silhouettes below the surface. In this hyper-accelerated and superficial political environment, Tingle suggests, our knowledge of modern political and institutional history has atrophied to a sketchy caricature. Even more damaging, she suggests that this amnesia among political, media and public service actors is cultivated and actively rewarded by a system in which methodical and deliberative debates over public policy have been supplanted by a fevered churn of catchy announceables, seven-second grabs and breathless "gotcha" moments.

Tingle saves her sharpest barbs for the brief, hysterical tenure of Prime Minister Abbott, whose reign hopefully marks the nadir of this kind of blindfold politics, but with Prime Minister Turnbull's page in history as yet unwritten, it is too soon to tell whether or not the tides described in this essay are turning, at least as far as the major parties are concerned.

The relentless erosion of the public sphere by private interests deserves further scrutiny, as the public sector has found itself increasingly contorted, downsized and restructured. While Tingle's essay mournfully describes the loss of institutional memory as a natural consequence of decades of perpetual overhaul and quickening political cycles, the public is also sold the assumption that lean, for-profit corporations will always deliver services more efficiently than lumbering, faceless bureaucracies. As the essay demonstrates, a little historical remembering does substantial damage to this lucrative conceit.

This is just one way in which our political culture now firmly rewards political amnesia. It has become an adaptive trait. I can't help but wonder how much that has to do with the convergence of the ALP and the Coalition towards some beige, neoliberal-infected political "centre" so that in some respects they are nearly indistinguishable. Political amnesia helps Labor insiders cope with the quiet abandonment of progressive positions when they move from Opposition to government, and it has certainly smoothed the conscience of the Coalition to forget that had their approach to the global financial crisis prevailed, Australia would probably have gone into a sharp recession. Principally, this cultivated amnesia helps all participants in the major parties stay sane when party positions change or reverse through some urgent expedient, rendering yesterday's strident rhetoric about Oceania awkwardly incompatible with today's talking points about Eastasia.

While precise details might be easily forgotten, the wearisome tenor of this fishbowl politics is having a marked effect on the electorate, which is now voting for non-major-party candidates in record numbers. The combined vote of the ALP and the Coalition has been in long decline, as voters are tempted towards independents and minor parties who, irrespective of their politics, at least appear to have a pulse. Thus the Senate now contains the largest number of crossbenchers in its history and functions from time to time as a genuinely deliberative chamber, a point alluded to briefly in the essay but probably worth further consideration.

The role of the internet also deserves another look. On the surface, social media platforms have quickened the pace of superficial political churn and deepened our tribal echo chambers, but there are countervailing tendencies that are more interesting. The internet is also a deep repository of political memory – anyone with a modicum of interest and access to a web browser can unearth historical parliamentary reports, statements, press clippings or tweets and pull them into the flow of today's conversation in a way that was impossible in the relatively recent past. The more conversational, many-to-many nature of the medium also acts as a counterweight to older-style broadcast politics, where rulers could more easily get away with assurances that, "We've always been at war with Eastasia." There are public engagement tools being brought into service in the United States and Europe that are bringing citizens ever closer to direct democracy, and the first pillar of such deliberative techniques is access to good information for all participants, which can't help but act as a solvent of the kind of cultivated ignorance described in the essay.

Political amnesia is hardly just an Australian phenomenon – the grotesque US Republican primaries provide one sharp example of that – but we do our forgetting in our own unique way. I can't help but feel that having swung so far in the direction laid out in Laura Tingle's essay, maybe the pendulum is at last heading back the other way. We'd best hope so.

Scott Ludlam

POLITICAL AMNESIA

Correspondence

Michael Keating and Stephen Sedgwick

We agree with much of Laura Tingle's perceptive analysis. We question, however, whether advice from the public service is now devalued because of its loss of institutional memory. We also question her conclusion that this memory loss stems from excessive staff mobility between agencies and too much contracting out, which necessarily reduce specialist skills and knowledge.

The number of separations from the Australian Public Service has remained pretty constant for a long time. Retrenchments are up but resignations are down in recent years, for example. As regards mobility between agencies, the overall rate is 1.6 per cent, which is neither high nor much changed in more than fifteen years. Moreover, among senior staff mobility seems to have fallen. Arguably it ought to be higher, since too many public servants can become stuck in their and their employer's comfort zone. Shifting between similar agencies can be a learning experience that challenges preconceptions, improves self-knowledge and encourages innovation. Indeed, Tingle approvingly cites the performance of the Department of Finance in the 1980s and 1990s, which pursued a policy of recruiting from other agencies – the average time spent in Finance by most of the subject matter experts was about two years.

When considering the impact of contracting out on institutional memory, Tingle cites the school-building and home-insulation programs. First, even those who criticise elements of their implementation need to acknowledge that both of these programs supported a lot of employment across the nation, arguably the key objective, and that the improvements in school infrastructure and energy savings are enduring and worthwhile. Second, it is not clear what actual experience of delivery the Australian government was meant to draw on, as it had *never* been directly engaged in these activities. (It needs to be remembered that the states, not the federal government, deliver the main public services, such as education, health, transport, building and construction and policing.) In the case of pink batts, the environment department acknowledged its lack of expertise and recommended that states or nationally operating contractors deliver the program. It was overruled in favour of delivery by "blokes in utes" – a government decision. Moreover, evidence was tendered to the royal commission that the government was advised (unfortunately not in writing) to delay implementation because of risks.

Finally, Treasury had advised the government to favour responses to the global financial crisis that could be rolled out quickly ("go hard, go early, go households") because it had examined what went wrong with the response to the 1990–91 recession. Back then emphasis was given to major infrastructure projects, which state premiers declared to be "shovel-ready", but in practice about two years elapsed before expenditure fully geared up, which was too late. In 2008–09, smaller projects spread across the country offered a much better chance of forestalling a feared recession.

Frankly we think Tingle very much overstates the role of contracting out in eroding institutional memory. What matters is that governance is designed to maximise the incentives for good performance; that agencies have access to relevant data so that they can evaluate performance; and how curious advisers are to understand their environment and how best to meet policy objectives. When employment services were outsourced in 1998, for example, great care was taken to capture performance information, which was intended to inform both policy and the allocation of future business among the private providers.

Ultimately, these are issues of organisational capability and culture, which in our experience can be undervalued even when the agency is directly responsible for delivery. Capability of this kind can be built in many ways. For example, in the 1980s and 1990s independent evaluation of all federal government programs was made mandatory. This was intended to force policy-makers to consider what does and doesn't work, and why. Unfortunately, independent evaluations are much less frequent these days, which may suggest that politicians or senior public servants don't want to risk receipt of information that reflects badly on their programs. Such attitudes can persist whether or not a program is outsourced.

Notwithstanding these qualifications, we do agree with Tingle that the role of the APS in giving policy advice (and especially unsolicited advice) has been diminished. So too has its capacity to engage in forward-looking strategic thinking. The critical issue is why such a gap exists. Is it, as some have argued, that successive governments have told senior managers that their job is "to do, not to think"? Is it because politics has become more polarised and personalised, with fewer continuous positions across governments? Is it that senior managers give priority to "the relationship" with the minister or the office over "speaking truth to power" and have lost the ability to have difficult conversations? Or is there a failure of communication – in one reviewed case, the senior managers of an agency argued that what the government wanted of them was, in effect, issues management, whereas current and previous ministers expressed concern about the same agency's lack of strategic focus. Or is the APS culture now so heavily task-focused (and, as some have argued, slimmed down) that there is little time for critical thinking or innovation, which undermines a culture of curiosity and engagement with ideas? This list of suggestions is far from exhaustive – but it has little to do with staff mobility or outsourcing.

We believe that public servants should be responsive to the government of the day, but they should be able to combine this with a capacity to warn and to suggest alternatives where necessary. Reforms in the 1980s were, inter alia, intended to make the APS more responsive, but unfortunately the pendulum now seems to have swung too far in that direction. Successive governments and the public service leadership probably share responsibility for this. As Tingle comments, "It is not just about politicisation. It is a result of politicians failing to value and preserve institutions."

Michael Keating and Stephen Sedgwick

POLITICAL AMNESIA

Response to Correspondence

Laura Tingle

Laments for the decline of our political discourse, of our institutions, have been a regular feature of the Australian political landscape in recent decades. But the germ of the idea at the heart of *Political Amnesia* came from elsewhere. Amid the appalling state of politics in the first half of 2015, many people were bemoaning the loss of a connection with "adult government." Labor in office had no idea what it was doing, the argument went, but then the Coalition won the 2013 election and rapidly appeared intent on proving to us that it had not a clue either.

In this vein, a feature of the often bizarre politics of the Abbott era which struck me – and others – was that the Coalition was repeating, almost move for move, all of Labor's political and policy mistakes.

I started to consider the issue of memory and why it seemed to have become so faulty in our politics. In turn, that made me think about the institutions which constitute our political world: the political parties and organs of executive government and the parliament, the public service and the media. I wondered whether, maybe, the bad politics came from a lack of memory and, in turn, what might have brought this about.

The themes of institutional memory loss and the decline of institutions are interwoven, of course. Writing the essay, I found it all too easy to stray occasionally into straightforward examination of institutions rather than what they can bring to our discourse because of their collective experience. And this is apparent in many of the responses to the essay – both some of those included here and those appearing in other forums.

The essay has struck a particularly powerful chord in the public service, often with more of a focus on the decline of the APS than on the decline of institutional memory per se.

Others have argued that we don't need to remember things because the world has changed so much that past lessons aren't relevant. I fear that some of those advocating this position may have cause later in life to blush at such bold assertions because they utterly miss the point of my argument.

My argument has never been that things were done well in the "olden days" and we ought to replicate what happened then. That would obviously be a ludicrous position. In the economic world, for example, the structures have been utterly transformed from those of a few decades ago.

Instead, the argument is about some very simple ideas: that knowing there are, or have been, alternative ways of approaching anything will make your deliberations better; that having different perspectives brings a creative tension to deliberation – for example, the tension between the public good and the political imperative.

Knowledge of alternatives and the existence of a vibrant creative tension both require strong institutions which are confident of their power base and place in the world. And the whole point of my essay is that what lies at the core of this confidence and vibrancy is knowledge and tradition. Their value does not lie in sentiment, but in the perspective they give on new ideas, and the way they enrich the capacities of the people who run our country and must deliver on those ideas.

Political Amnesia has sought to remind people of this value, and I believe it has helped to start a much-needed debate about how the balance of power, influence and ideas in our institutions has shifted in the past few decades. Most importantly, it has begun a debate about whether we need to change this balance for the better – not to go back to the past, but to secure a more vibrant future.

Laura Tingle

Tarah Barzanji was an adviser to Prime Minister Kevin Rudd and a common-wealth public servant. She is now a manager at the economics consultancy AlphaBeta.

Allan Behm is the author of No, Minister: So You Want To Be a Chief of Staff? and a commentator on international and security affairs. He was Greg Combet's chief of staff in the defence materiel, climate change and industry portfolios.

Graham Evans was Bob Hawke's first chief of staff, secretary of the Departments of Primary Industries and Energy (1987–88), Transport and Communications (1988–93) and Defence (1993–95), Vice-President External Affairs of BHP Billiton and founding chair of the Victorian Competition and Efficiency Commission.

Bernie Fraser was secretary of the Treasury (1984–89), governor of the Reserve Bank (1989–96) and, more recently, chairman of the board of the Climate Change Authority.

Michael Keating was secretary of the Departments of Employment and Industrial Relations (1983–86), Finance (1986–91) and Prime Minister and Cabinet (1991–96).

Scott Ludlam is a Greens senator, representing Western Australia.

George Megalogenis has thirty years' experience in the media, including over a decade in the federal parliamentary press gallery. His book *The Australian*

Moment won the 2013 Prime Minister's Award for non-fiction and formed the basis for the ABC TV series *Making Australia Great.* His most recent book is *Australia's Second Chance* and he is also author of *Faultlines, The Longest Decade* and the Quarterly Essay *Trivial Pursuit: Leadership and the End of the Reform Era.*

John Quiggin is a professor of economics at the University of Queensland and a member of the board of the Climate Change Authority. His book *Zombie Economics* was published in 2010.

Jennifer Rayner is a federal political adviser and the author of Generation Less: How *Australia Is Cheating the Young.*

Stephen Sedgwick was secretary of the Departments of Finance (1992–97), Employment, Education, Training and Youth Affairs (1997–98) and Education (1998–2002). From 2009 to 2014 he was APS Commissioner.

Anne Tiernan is a professor in the School for Government and International Relations at Griffith University and the co-author of *The Gatekeepers: Lessons from Prime Ministers' Chief of Staff.*

Laura Tingle is political editor of the Australian Financial Review. She won Walkley awards in 2005 and 2011. In 2010 she was shortlisted for the John Button Prize for political writing. She appears regularly on ABC-TV's *Insiders.* Her two Quarterly Essays are

Political Amnesia: How We Forgot How to Govern and *Great Expectations: Government, Entitlement and an Angry Nation.*

Amanda Walsh worked in the Australian Public Service from 1996 to 2010, including several years in the Department of Foreign Affairs and Trade. She is currently a project manager at the peak advocacy organisation Early Childhood Australia. She completed a PhD in politics in 2015.

FORTHCOMING ISSUES:

James Brown on Going to War June 2016

Don Watson on the US Election September 2016

***

***

ECONOBABBLE
HOW TO DECODE POLITICAL SPIN AND ECONOMIC NONSENSE
Richard Denniss
REDBACK QUARTERLY

***

Available where all good books are sold.
blackincbooks.com

Back Cover Material

In this urgent essay, George Megalogenis argues that Australia risks becoming globalisation's next and most unnecessary victim. The next shock, whenever it comes, will find us with our economic guard down, and a political system that has shredded its authority.

Megalogenis outlines the challenge for Malcolm Turnbull and his government. Our tax system is unfair and we have failed to invest in infrastructure and education. Both sides of politics are clinging defensively to an old model because it tells them a reassuring story of Australian success. But that model has been exhausted by capitalism's extended crisis and the end of the mining boom. Trusting to the market has left us with gridlocked cities, growing inequality and a corporate sector that feels no obligation to pay tax. It is time to redraw the line between market and state.

Balancing Act is a passionate look at the politics of change and renewal, and a bold call for active government. It took World War II to provide the energy and focus for the reconstruction that laid the foundation for modern Australia. Will it take another crisis to prompt a new reconstruction?

"Australia is in transition. Saying it is easy. The panic kicks in when we are compelled to describe what the future might look like. There is no complacent middle to aim at. We will either catch

the next wave of prosperity, or finally succumb to the Great Recession."

George Megalogenis, *Balancing Act*

George Megalogenis has thirty years' experience in the media, including over a decade in the federal parliamentary press gallery. His book *The Australian Moment* won the 2013 Prime Minister's Award for non-fiction and formed the basis for the ABC TV series *Making Australia Great*. His most recent book is *Australia's Second Chance* and he is also author of *Faultlines,The Longest Decade* and QE40, *Trivial Pursuit.*

QUARTERLY ESSAY presents significant contributions to the general debate. Each issue contains a single essay written at a length of about 25,000 words. It aims to present the widest range of political, intellectual and cultural opinion.

Made in the USA
Monee, IL
05 November 2026

67811469R10096